LIV SPENCER

TAYLOR SWIFT

ECW PRESS

INTRODUCTION

In the not-too-distant pop-music past, a superstar with chart-topping records, shelves full of awards, and sold-out headlining tours seemed as remote to her millions of admirers as a star in the night sky. Rarely communicating directly with her fans, a celebrity kept in touch through media interviews and public appearances. Some pop stars still keep their distance today. Not Taylor Swift. Even in the social media era, Taylor stands out: from blog posts to video clips to tweets, she is in almost constant contact with the Taylor Nation, hugging fans at meet-and-greets before her concerts and always finding the time for an autograph or a photo. As in her confessional lyrics, this platinum-haired and platinum-selling singer-songwriter isn't afraid to share her real self with the world. A crucial part of Taylor's success has been her authenticity; it's easy to feel Taylor could be your best friend, one you admire for her relentless dedication and hard work.

Ever since she was a little girl in Pennsylvania listening to "uncool" country music, Taylor has single-mindedly pursued her dreams and — song by song, fan by fan, and city by city — she's made them a reality. She's emerged as not only a hit songwriter and dynamite performer, but as a savvy businesswoman who is actively involved in every aspect of her career from tour design to product partnerships to promotional strategy. She is careful about her personal life and her public image, but isn't afraid to experiment musically, to allow her sound to change and grow as she does. For all those reasons, an expanded and updated edition of this book was seriously in order. Here Taylor's journey is chronicled — her childhood, her loving and supportive family, her first attempts at getting a record deal as a precocious pre-teen, her songs, her videos, her friends, and her ever-growing list of accomplishments. What emerges is a portrait of a young woman who never, never, never gives up — and has succeeded in writing her own fairytale.

CHAPTER 1

GROWING UP SWIFTLY

On December 13, 1989, the number-one song topping the charts was Billy Joel's baby-boomer anthem "We Didn't Start the Fire." Little did anyone know, in the small borough of Wyomissing, Pennsylvania, a spark was being born in the form of Taylor Alison Swift, who would burn up the charts less than two decades later.

Taylor's savvy parents — Andrea Swift, a successful businesswoman, and Scott Swift, a stockbroker — wanted to make sure their daughter would have every advantage possible, and named her appropriately. Andrea reasoned that future employers wouldn't know if Taylor was a boy or a girl if they saw her name on a business card or résumé. Taylor explained to *Rolling Stone*, "She wanted me to be a business person in a business world." The platinum-selling singer-songwriter may not work in a boardroom, but there's no doubt Andrea Swift is anything but disappointed.

In Wyomissing, Taylor grew up on an 11-acre Christmas tree farm, which was the family's secondary business. The farm was also home to several cats and seven horses. Taylor was a young equestrian and rode horses competitively as a child. Taylor remembered, "I was raised on a little farm and for me when I was little, it was the biggest place in the world. And it was the most magical, wonderful place in the world." She spent her time "running free and going anywhere I wanted in my head." When she was two, she got a partner to play with when Andrea and Scott brought brother Austin home to join the Swift family. When Taylor was four, Andrea decided to set her career aside and focus on her family.

As Taylor shared in "The Best Day," her love song for her family, the Swifts are a close-knit bunch. Telling *Girls' Life* about her mom, Taylor explained, "She's one of my best friends. She's always, always around. She's the person in my life who will just literally look me in the eye and say, 'Look, snap out of it.' You know? And I need that person." Taylor also recognizes that her mother's influence was a major factor in achieving her astonishing success: "She totally raised me to be logical and practical. I was brought up with such a strong woman in my life and I think that had a lot to do with me not wanting to do anything halfway."

The special bond between mother and daughter doesn't go unnoticed by Scott Swift, who told the *Tennessean*: "People keep saying to me, 'The relationship between Andrea and Taylor is something pretty special.' That is amazing. There aren't too many mother and daughters who work together as a business unit the way those two do." And while Scott may not be constantly by Taylor's side now, he still plays a major role in his daughter's life. Andrea's parenting approach is firm though loving, realistic, and honest, while Scott is a softie. "My dad is just a big teddy bear who tells me that everything I do is perfect," said Taylor. Like his wife, Scott passes on his wisdom to his daughter, helping her make sound financial decisions about her career independently. "Business-wise, he's brilliant," said Taylor. "I'm constantly getting business advice and what to invest in. I think you should be in charge of every single aspect of your career."

As a parenting team, Andrea and Scott balance each other out. Taylor told the *Tennessean*, "I have a logical, practical, realistic mother, and a head-in-the-clouds, kind and friendly, optimistic father. And so I'm a dreamer, and my imagination goes to places where love lasts forever and everything is covered in glitter, and that's from my dad's personality. Every time I walk off stage, he tells me how much he loved it, or how he was standing at the soundboard, crying. But my mom, she'll tell me exactly what she saw."

While Taylor may get her confidence and her business sense from her parents, her musical talent comes from someone else: her late maternal grandmother, Marjorie Finlay, a successful opera singer. Taylor reminisced, "I can remember her singing, the thrill of it. She was one of my first inspirations," and she elaborated to the *Sunday Times*: "She would have these wonderful parties at her house, and she would get up and sing. She always wanted to be onstage, whether she was in the middle of her living room or in church; she just loved it. And when she would walk into a room, everyone would look at her, no matter what; she had this 'thing,' this 'it factor.' I always noticed it — that she was different from everyone else." Marjorie traveled with her husband, who built oil rigs around the world, and she performed in places like Singapore, Puerto Rico, and Vietnam. When Andrea was 10, the family settled in America. Marjorie appeared in operas like *The Bartered Bride* and *The Barber of Seville* and musicals such as *West Side Story*. Scott Swift notices similarities that go beyond musical ability between his daughter and his mother-in-law: "The two of them had some sort of magic where they could walk into a room and remember everybody's name. Taylor has the grace and the same physique of Andrea's mother. Andrea's mother had this unique quality; if she was going into a room, literally everybody loved Marjorie."

Taylor's legacy from her grandmother appeared at a very young age. She had an uncanny ability to memorize songs, and Taylor remembers that at age three or four, "I would come out of these Disney movies and I'd be singing every single song from the movie on the car ride home, word for word. And my parents noticed that once I had run out of words I would just make up my own." Taylor admitted, "I was that annoying kid who ran around singing for random strangers."

The young girl was hooked on more than just singing; Taylor was addicted to stories too. Taylor told Katie Couric, "All I wanted to do was talk and all I wanted to do was hear stories. I would drive my mom insane driving down the road [with her]." Like other children, Taylor demanded stories at bedtime, but rather than reading the same books over and over, Taylor insisted on originals. "I refused to go to bed without a story. And I always wanted to hear a new one," she said. No wonder Andrea admitted her energetic youngster "had the potential to be exhausting."

It wasn't too long before Taylor started making up her own stories. She told the *Washington Post*, "Writing is pretty involuntary to me. I'm always writing." Taylor's love of language "started with poetry, trying to figure out the perfect combination of words, with the perfect amount of syllables and the perfect rhyme to make it completely pop off the page." She loved Dr. Seuss and Shel Silverstein, and told *Rolling Stone*: "I noticed early on that poetry was something that just stuck in my head and I was replaying those rhymes and try[ing] to think of my own. In English, the only thing I wanted to do was poetry and all the other kids were like, 'Oh, man. We have to write poems again?' and I would have a three-page long poem." In the fourth grade she won a national poetry contest for her composition "Monster in My Closet." She even wrote a 350 page novel during a summer vacation. Andrea

A young Taylor as Kim in a children's theater production of *Bye Bye Birdie*.

remembered, "She wrote all the time. If music hadn't worked out, I think she'd be going off to college to take journalism classes or trying to become a novelist."

Beyond music and stories, Taylor demonstrated one more quality at a young age that would prove useful on her rise to superstardom: she was at ease in front of the camera and knew how to strike a pose that even Tyra Banks would call fierce. Andrea told British magazine *Sugar*, "I got photos taken for family Christmas cards when Taylor was five. She was really posing. The photographer told me I should take her to L.A. to model, but I'm so glad I didn't." Millions of fans are glad she didn't too.

ENTERING THE SPOTLIGHT

When Taylor was around 10, she decided she wanted to follow in her grandmother's footsteps and sing in front of an audience. She auditioned for the local children's theater company a week after she saw its production of *Charlie and the Chocolate Factory*. Since she was tall, Taylor was given the lead roles, and played such memorable parts as Sandy in *Grease*, Kim in *Bye Bye Birdie*, and Maria in *The Sound of Music*, but Taylor admitted, "My singing sounded a lot more country than Broadway." And though Taylor liked being onstage, what really captured her heart was performing karaoke at the cast parties. The

songstress explained, "Singing country music on that karaoke machine was my favorite thing in the world." She sang the Shania Twain, Dixie Chicks, and Faith Hill songs that she'd been listening to since a LeAnn Rimes album got her hooked on country music at age six. Her inspiring performances didn't go unnoticed, and Taylor remembered, "One day, somebody turned to my mom and said, 'You know, she really ought to be singing country music.'" Taylor added, "It kind of occurred to all of us at the same time that that's what I needed to be doing."

Taylor started scouring the phone book for more places to perform. One of her regular spots was the Pat Garrett Roadhouse in Strausstown, Pennsylvania, which held frequent karaoke contests. Taylor started going every week, taking her parents along with her. "They were kind of embarrassed by it, I

guess," remembered Taylor. "This little girl singing in this smoky bar. But they knew how much it meant to me so they went along with it." A year and a half later, her performance of LeAnn Rimes' "Big Deal" earned her not only the prestige of being karaoke champion, but also a spot opening for Grammy-winner and country legend Charlie Daniels at the amphitheater across the street. In this case, "opening" meant that Taylor went on at 10 a.m. while Charlie Daniels played at 8 p.m. Nevertheless, it was a pretty amazing feat for an 11-year-old.

Demonstrating business smarts that would make her parents proud, Taylor discovered that another way to reach a large audience was to perform the national anthem at sports games. She sent demo tapes out everywhere. She sang regularly for her local minor league baseball team, the Reading Phillies, and would take whatever other gigs she could get from local garden club meetings all the way up to the U.S. Open tennis tournament when she was 12. "I figured out that if you could sing that one song, you could get in front of 20,000 people without even having a record deal," Taylor told *Rolling Stone*. One of the highlights of her anthem-singing career came at age 11 when she sang at a 76ers game. Jay-Z was sitting courtside and, after her performance, the famous rapper and hip hop mogul gave young T-Swizzle a high-five. "I bragged about that for, like, a year straight," Taylor admitted.

As her career progressed, Taylor kept singing the anthem, though her eventual record deal helped get her in front of considerably larger audiences. She performed "The Star-Spangled Banner" at game three of the

2008 World Series between the Philadelphia Phillies and the Tampa Bay Rays. Even though she'd sung the anthem hundreds of times, performing at such an important game was still a little daunting. Taylor explained, "The national anthem is not as challenging range-wise, because I've been doing it for so long. The challenge for me is the utter silence that comes over 40,000 people in a baseball stadium and you're the only one singing it. . . . It's a really surreal moment for me."

But before she was a household name performing at one of the nation's most important sporting events, Taylor was just trying to find an audience. She watched a TV special about one of her heroes, Faith Hill, who talked about making it in Nashville, the home of country music. Taylor realized, "That's the promised land for country music. That's where I need to go."

Taylor made a demo tape of her singing the country songs she had grown to love backed by karaoke tracks, and convinced her mom to take her to the legendary city on a spring break trip. Andrea packed up Taylor and Austin and they drove down to Nashville. Taylor walked into the record-company offices on Music Row, handed them her demo, and boldly announced, "Hi, I'm Taylor. I'm 11. I really want a record deal." But as charming as the aspiring star's courage was, the companies weren't wooed. "Basically all the record companies went, 'Ah, how cute. She's just a little kid.' [and] 'Give up your dreams. Go home and come back when you're 18,'" recalled Taylor. "I chose not to hear that. I wasn't prepared to accept that I wasn't a relevant artist until I was 18." The record companies steadfastly believed that young people didn't listen to country music. Taylor was frequently told, "The country music demographic is 35-year-old females and those are the only people who listen to country music," but she remembered, "I just kept thinking that can't be true. That can't be accurate because I listen to country music and I know there have to be other girls everywhere who listen to country music. . . . So I kept trying because I didn't believe that there was just one tiny demographic." Of course, that younger demographic *did* exist, and while the record execs might not have known it yet, Taylor did, and in a few short years, she would prove it to them.

GUITAR HERO, SOCIAL OUTCAST

Returning home to Wyomissing, Taylor knew she had to do something to distinguish herself from all the other wannabe performers, and she came up with two ways she could do that: she'd learn to play the guitar and she'd write her own music. Taylor explained, "There are a lot of gorgeous voices and beautiful women in Nashville, so I had to figure out a way to stand out. I thought if I could walk into an audition and play a song that I had written, then I'd stand out. And that has really made a difference."

Taylor had a guitar already — she'd received an electric guitar at age eight, and had actually started taking lessons but she had been discouraged quickly. It was a less formal teacher who got her playing for good; she learned her first three chords from a guy who came by to fix the family's computer. Ten minutes later, she'd written her first song, "Lucky

You." Each week, the computer guy would teach his young pupil a few more chords. By age 12, she was playing guitar four hours a day, every day. In classic T-Swift style, she decided to play on the more challenging 12-string model, as opposed to a six-string, because her first teacher had told her she wouldn't be able to do it. She told *Teen Vogue*, "I actually learned on a 12-string, purely because some guy told me that I'd never be able to play it, that my fingers were too small. Anytime someone tells me that I can't do something, I want to do it more." Andrea was floored by her daughter's commitment: "Her fingers would crack from so much playing. She was driven beyond anything I had ever witnessed."

Taylor's single-minded commitment to music may have wowed her mother, but it wasn't something that made her popular at school. The other kids made fun of her bleeding fingers and her love for country music, and were jealous of the attention she received for performing. She remembered, "I kind of started to live in fear when I would sing the national anthem at the 76ers game. If there was a write-up about it the next day in our local paper, I knew it was gonna be a bad day at school for me." A group of popular girls who used to be friendly with Taylor decided to exclude her: "When I'd sit down at the lunch table, they'd get up and move. Or, as I was setting up my equipment to sing karaoke at the town summer festival, the kids would shout horrible things." Andrea recalled, "She was shunned. After school, I'd hear what nightmare had occurred that day, what awful thing was done to her. I'd have to pick her up off the floor."

The budding performer also found her priorities were hugely different from those of her classmates: "All the girls at school were going to sleepovers and breaking into their parents' liquor cabinets on the weekend, and all I wanted to do was go to festivals and sing karaoke music." Taylor still picks music over drinking and parties, and since making that decision in junior high, the songstress has retained the same values — she won't let anything compromise her music career.

Despite rejecting the more rebellious aspects of the social scene, the outsider still desperately wanted to fit in, and Taylor tried to act just like everyone else. She even attempted to tame her curly locks, imitating the straight-haired look of the popular girls. "I tried so hard to be like everybody else and do what they did and like the things they liked," she said. "I tried so hard and it didn't work. They still didn't want to be friends with me. . . . So I found that trying to be like everyone else doesn't work." Looking back, Taylor can see what drove her need to conform: insecurity. "Whatever makes you different in middle school makes you uncool somehow. I hate that. I think that one thing I realized, after the fact, was that everybody was insecure. Maybe it wasn't the same insecurity that I had, but it's always something. It's funny how after you get out of middle school, the thing that you were the most insecure about can be the thing that sets you apart." With the wisdom of a few more years and a wildly successful career, Taylor offered comfort to other teens who may be going through the same thing, saying, "The only place where it's cool to be the same as everyone else is junior high." Trapped in her school's hallways, Taylor eventually came to terms with the fact that she'd never be in-crowd material, and embraced what made her special, even if that meant standing out, and ultimately, standing apart from everyone else.

The straight-A student found herself in a lonely position on the outside, observing rather than joining in the regular goings-on of middle school. She recalled, "I was facing a lot of things at school where I found myself on the outside looking in. I was not included. I would go to school some days, a lot of days, and not know who I was going to talk to. And that's a really terrifying thing for somebody who's 12." Luckily, Taylor had an outlet for feeling alone and excluded; she channeled it into her songwriting. She wrote the song "The Outside" when she was 12 to capture that feeling, writing, "Nobody ever lets me in / I can still see you, this ain't the best view / On the outside looking in." Her point of view as an outsider became a great source of material for Taylor's songs: "The people around me provided all the inspiration I needed. Everything I wrote [at that time] came from that experience, what I observed happening around me."

Later in her career, Taylor would learn to be grateful to the people who had made her life so miserable and given her so much fuel for her songwriting. She realized, "The only thing I can do is look back and thank [those classmates]. If I hadn't been so driven to music because I didn't have anyone to hang out with, if I hadn't written songs because I didn't have anyone to talk to, I wouldn't be sitting here right now."

But at the time, hurting from rejection and loneliness, she channeled everything into her music; writing songs became like a diary for Taylor, and it still is. As her mother told the *New York Times*, "She simply has to write songs. It's how she filters her life." Taylor was able to turn her schoolyard rejection into something bigger, something that brought her closer to her goal of having a record deal. Despite being a dreamer, Taylor knew achieving her goal wouldn't be easy, and that she had to keep writing, practicing, and performing to make it happen. Part of this practicality came from her mother, who, Taylor explained, "never said to me, 'Taylor, you're gonna be famous someday.'" Taylor continued, "There are so many moms who tell their kids that. But my mom has always been practical. She didn't know if I would succeed. She'd say, 'If you want a chance at this, you've got to work real-ly, really hard.'" And so Taylor did, writing and practicing constantly and performing at all the music festivals, karaoke competitions, and national-anthem gigs she could fit in around her school schedule. Taylor told *Cosmo Girl*, "The reason I was so driven was that I didn't expect that anything would just happen for me. But that doubt fueled me to work harder. My attitude was the opposite of people who are like, 'It's gonna happen for me. It's gonna happen for me.' My mantra was always 'It's not gonna happen for me. Go out and play the show or it won't happen.'"

One such show made a huge difference in Taylor's career — the U.S. Open, one of the four most prestigious tennis tournaments in the world. Taylor belted out "The Star-Spangled Banner" in front of a massive crowd of over 20,000 tennis fans. Among them was Dan Dymtrow, then manager of Britney Spears. Impressed with Taylor's talent, Dymtrow took

her on as a client and worked to promote the young artist. Dymtrow helped 13-year-old Taylor get a development deal with RCA Records in Nashville. It seemed like a huge step forward, but after holding onto her for a year, Taylor's contract came up for review. Taylor performed for RCA bigwigs, and the label decided to shelve her rather than have her make a record immediately. "That means they want to watch you, but they're not promising to make an album with you," explained Taylor. "Kind of like a guy who wants to date you but not be your boyfriend." It wasn't enough for the ambitious teen, who was in a hurry to share her music with the world. "I genuinely felt that I was running out of time. I'd written all these songs and I wanted to capture these years of my life on an album while they still represented what I was going through." But more than anything, Taylor was disappointed that RCA didn't have faith in her potential, so she walked away from the deal — a bold move for a young singer without a fallback plan. She recalled, "I figured if they didn't believe in me then, they weren't ever going to believe in me."

Taylor still believed in herself, and she worked at convincing her family to make a permanent move to the heartland of country music — Nashville, Tennessee. Her persistence paid off, and before Taylor's freshmen year the entire Swift family moved south for a fresh start in Music City, USA.

CHAPTER 2

NEXT STOP, NASHVILLE

Leaving Pennsylvania behind wasn't too difficult for Taylor, who was literally moving closer to her Nashville dream and away from her bullying classmates, but it required a bigger sacrifice from the rest of her uprooted family, especially her father, who had to transfer his business. Nevertheless, the Swifts never put pressure on Taylor. She told *Self* magazine, "I knew I was the reason they were moving. But they tried to put no pressure on me. They were like, 'Well, we need a change of scenery anyway' and 'I love how friendly people in Tennessee are.'" Andrea had faith in her daughter and trusted her intentions: "It was never about 'I want to be famous.' Taylor never uttered those words. It was about moving to a place where she could write with people she could learn from."

Taylor was glad her family trusted her instincts. "Sometimes you don't have a sure answer as to where you're going to go or where you're going to end up, but if you have an instinct as to where you don't need to be, you need to follow it and my parents let me make that decision completely," recalled Taylor.

She didn't have a label anymore, but she had experience working with one. In 2004, Taylor was featured in an Abercrombie & Fitch "rising stars" campaign and one of her songs appeared on a compilation album, the Maybelline-produced *Chicks with Attitude*. "The Outside," the song she'd written about feeling excluded in middle school, had found a temporary home.

It wasn't long before Taylor found a home as a songwriter at Sony/ATV Records. She was the youngest songwriter they'd ever hired, which is an impressive feat, but Taylor knew

she'd still have to prove herself by acting with maturity beyond her years. "I knew the stereotype people had when they heard the words '14-year-old girl' was that I wasn't going to do the hard work, and I wanted people to know that I was," Taylor emphasized. "One of my first songwriting sessions was with [accomplished songwriter and producer] Brett Beavers, and I walked in with 15 different starts to songs. I love being prepared and I love organization, and I need people to know that I care and that this is important to me."

Being a professional songwriter meant that Taylor had to lead a sort of double life, going to high school in Hendersonville during the day and writing songs in the afternoons in downtown Nashville, less than 20 miles away. Taylor called her life back then "a really weird existence," and elaborated, "I was a teenager during the day when I was at school, and then at night it was like I was 45. My mom would pick me up from school and I'd go downtown and sit and write songs with these hit songwriters."

The social politics of high school in Tennessee turned out to be very similar to those of junior high in Pennsylvania, but luckily for Taylor, there was one major difference that made school tolerable — a great friend. Taylor met red-haired Abigail Anderson in ninth grade English, when the new girl wowed the class with her sophisticated composition. "We were the ones in the back of the class saying negative things about *Romeo and Juliet* because we were so bitter toward that emotion at the time," recalled Abigail. Neither girl was a member of the popular clique, so the pair made their own rules, focusing on

WELCOME TO MUSIC CITY, USA

With her songwriting gig, Taylor was part of the rich music history of Nashville, a city that has been home to music publishing since 1824 when *Western Harmony*, a book of hymns, was produced there. It was in the 1920s that Nashville music really began to flourish with the opening of the Grand Ole Opry. In the '40s and '50s, "Music Row" developed as Capitol Records and RCA first opened outposts in the capital and every other major label followed suit. Today, Nashville's 16th and 17th Avenues South are home to recording studios and labels galore.

The "Nashville Sound," a blend of a pop music sensibility with the traditional storytelling of folk and country artists, was popularized in the 1950s by legends like Jim Reeves, Patsy Cline, and Eddy Arnold. Its legacy can be heard in Taylor's song-crafting style that mixes infectious melodies with memorable tales rooted in real-life experiences.

As Nashville recording artist Elvis Presley helped make rock 'n' roll a craze, sales of country music albums dropped, and "crossing over" from country to mainstream listeners became hugely important for country artists. In the 1980s, the star of country crossover was the Queen of Country Music herself, Dolly Parton, whose music and personality made her a household name from coast to coast. Alongside the queen was the King of Country, George Strait, who trails only the Beatles and Elvis Presley for the number of hit albums he's released. Now in his sixties, he holds the record for the most number-one singles of any artist in any genre, and he's always stayed true to a traditional honky-tonk sound. The '80s also saw the rise of hugely successful country acts such as Alabama and Reba McEntire.

Like a certain blonde teenager would 20 years later, Garth Brooks started as a Nashville songwriter before rapidly taking country music by storm with songs like "The Thunder Rolls" in the 1990s, bringing with him the "new country" sound, over 36 top 10 hits, record-breaking tours, and millions of albums sold. Garth's audience stretched well beyond the traditional country music boundaries. It's no surprise that Taylor Swift has called Garth Brooks her "role model."

But it was the female country musicians of the '90s that most influenced young Taylor, and it all started with then-14-year-old LeAnn Rimes' 1996 album *Blue*, which Taylor heard when she was just six years old. Recalled Taylor, "LeAnn Rimes was my first impression of country music . . . I just really loved how she could be making music and having a career at such a young age." Taylor "started listening to female country artists nonstop" from legends like Patsy Cline, Loretta Lynn, Tammy Wynette, and Dolly Parton to the stars of the '90s like Shania Twain, Faith Hill, and the Dixie Chicks. As Taylor explained to *Rolling Stone*, "I saw that Shania Twain brought this independence and this crossover appeal; I saw that

Dolly Parton, Tim McGraw, and Faith Hill at the 2000 ACM Award nominations. Taylor loves Dolly's response to male fans who interrupt quiet performance moments: "Some guy screamed from the crowd, 'I love you, Dolly!' and she goes, 'I thought I told you to stay in the truck!'"

Faith Hill brought this classic old-school glamour and beauty and grace; and I saw that the Dixie Chicks brought this complete 'we don't care what you think' quirkiness, and I loved what these women were able to do and what they were able to bring to country music."

Taylor has measured her career's progress by following in the footsteps of the legends who sang the music she grew up listening to. At a Bakersville, California, show shortly after Taylor's first album came out, the son of the late country legend Buck Owens presented her with a guitar: "I was on stage in front of 5,000 people and Buck Owens' son came out on stage with the red-white-and-blue guitar. Buck used to give them to [musicians] that he really respected, and [his son] said that this was the first one they had given away since we lost Buck. It blew my mind. I got really, really emotional. It was just so different than any other sort of respect. It was being approved and embraced by a country legend."

Another early career milestone for Taylor was the opportunity to play a show at the historic Grand Ole Opry. GAC filmed the experience (it's included on the deluxe version of her self-titled album). Taylor recounted, "There's this circle in the middle of the stage. It's like everybody from Patsy Cline to Keith Urban to LeAnn Rimes to me, now, have stood in this circle." At that moment, walking in the footsteps of country music's greats, Taylor knew she'd made it.

what they actually cared about rather than what other people did. For Taylor, that was music; for Abigail, competitive swimming: "When I was a freshman, I knew I wanted to swim in college, at a Division 1 school, and she knew that she wanted to go on tour." Such focus set the girls apart from their classmates, and bonded them together. Taylor explained to the *New York Times*, "It just dawned on me that I had to love being different or else I was going to end up being dark and angry and frustrated by school." Being different meant staying away from the popular-girl party scene, which Taylor had already decided didn't appeal to her. Taylor told *Glamour*, "I remember seeing girls crying in the bathroom every Monday about what they did at a party that weekend. I never wanted to be that girl."

MUSIC & LYRICS

Now that she was in the home of country music and had a songwriting contract, Taylor didn't abandon her earlier confessional style to start writing about stereotypical country music subjects. "I don't sing about tractors and hay bales and things like that because that's not really the way that I grew up. But I do sing about the lessons I've learned," Taylor explained. She wanted to write for people her age, those country-music fans the labels told her didn't exist but she knew did — they were just waiting for songs they could relate to. "I don't try to write for older than I am and I don't try and write for younger than I am. I write in real time," noted the songwriter.

These real-time songs are, above all,

personal and honest. They're about Taylor's feelings, her friends, her dreams, her heartbreak. She told *Seventeen*, "Honesty is a big part of my writing, because when I was younger and fell in love with songs I'd hear, I would always wonder who that song was about. It would totally have broken my heart to know it wasn't about anyone and was just written so it could be on the radio."

Now that she was at Hendersonville High, Taylor was accumulating all kinds of new material. She had her first flirtations with romance, and Taylor started to write the songs she'd become most famous for — songs about boys, love, and heartbreak. Since she is unafraid to name names, some of Taylor's early boyfriends are well known to her fans. These songs were a way for her to process her feelings and sometimes she directly addressed the person who inspired her words: "The only thing I think about when I'm writing a song is the person I'm writing the song about. Music is very confessional to me. It's a chance for me to say things I wouldn't be brave enough to say to the person's face."

Taylor's songs may be specific, but as millions of fans can attest, that doesn't mean they're not relatable. At first this came as a surprise to the young songwriter, who remembers, "I thought because my songs were so personal that nobody would be able to relate to them. . . . But apparently they were more significant to more people than just me." As it turns out, though the names may be different, the experiences Taylor writes about are fairly universal. Taylor reasoned, "The hardest thing about heartbreak is feeling like you're alone, and that the other person doesn't really care. But when you hear a song about it, you realize you're not alone — because the person who wrote it went through the same thing. That's what makes songs about heartbreak so relatable."

Because her inspiration came from immediate feelings and emotions, Taylor learned to write anytime and anywhere, not just in her after-school sessions at Sony. Stuck in class, she'd escape to the bathroom to record a melody on her cell phone, or scribble down lyrics alongside her lecture notes! Taylor admitted, "When teachers conducted random notebook checks they'd be freaked out — but they learned to deal with me." If inspiration came outside of class, she'd use anything at hand to capture the words before she lost them. "I've seen her pull out a Kleenex and write a song on it," Abigail revealed.

Taylor doesn't write all her songs single-handedly. In fact, in those early Nashville days she met one very important collaborator: Liz Rose. Liz started in the industry with her own music publishing company, which she sold in 2001 to focus more seriously on her writing. It turned out to be a great career choice. Since then she's penned hits sung by country stars such as Trisha Yearwood, Bonnie Raitt, Tim McGraw, and Kellie Pickler. But Liz's collaboration with Taylor would prove to be her most prolific and successful. When the pair met, Liz instantly saw something exceptional in Taylor: "Even then, you knew she was going to do something. She was so driven and so talented."

Many fruitful songwriting sessions followed; Liz shares the writing credit on seven songs on Taylor's self-titled debut album and

Taylor embraces Liz Rose as they collect a Grammy for Best Country Song on January 31, 2010.

four on *Fearless*. She helped write hits like "You Belong with Me," "Teardrops on My Guitar," and "White Horse." Liz humbly gives most of the credit to her young protégé: "My sessions with Taylor were some of the easiest I've ever done. Basically, I was just her editor. She'd write about what happened to her in school that day. She had such a clear vision of what she was trying to say. And she'd come in with some of the most incredible hooks." The elder songwriter elaborated, "She's a genius, coming in with ideas and a melody. She'd come in and write with this old lady and I never second-guessed her. I respect her a lot."

As Taylor was writing up a storm, she also recorded demos with a producer, Nathan Chapman, who was also just starting his career and was working in "a shack behind the publishing company," according to Taylor. She knew that Nathan was the right producer for her music, saying "I just fell in love with what he did with my songs." Like her collaboration with Liz Rose, Taylor's partnership with Nathan would continue through her career, and she would take the new producer with her on her rise to the top.

SONGBIRD AT THE BLUEBIRD

With hundreds of hours of guitar playing and songwriting under her belt, Taylor was looking for a chance to show off her talents to the country music elite, and it came in the form of a showcase at Nashville's famous Bluebird Café. The café auditions performers for songwriters' nights, and those who are very successful can be booked for a showcase event that draws local industry professionals

hunting for new talent. A major country star had gotten his big break at the Bluebird: in 1987 a young Garth Brooks was discovered there and signed by Capitol Records after a showcase performance.

On Taylor's night to shine, she took the stage and played an acoustic set, and when she looked out at the audience, she noticed one person who was completely absorbed in the music, listening with his eyes closed to take it all in. "He was listening better than anyone in the room," remembered Taylor. That person was Scott Borchetta, a former executive at a Nashville division of Universal Music Group, who Taylor had met once before, playing a few songs for the exec before he left his DreamWorks Nashville office. "I was just smitten on the spot. It was like a lightening bolt," he told Great American Country.

After the show, Scott approached Taylor, and told her, "I have good news and I have bad news. . . . The good news is that I want to sign you to a record deal. The bad news is that I'm no longer with Universal Records." But Scott Borchetta had a plan for his own label and told the young songwriter, "I want you to wait for me . . . I'm working on something." Taylor remembered, "The way he said it convinced me that there was something going on that I wanted to be a part of."

An essential part of their deal was that Taylor would get to write all the songs that would appear on her albums. A larger label might have forced her to record tracks penned by other songwriters, but Taylor refused to compromise on what had been the foundation of her career. She told the *Sunday Times*, "It would have really taken a lot of the wind out

A SHORT HISTORY OF BIG MACHINE RECORDS

Scott Borchetta got his first taste of the music business at a young age, working in the mail-room of his father's independent promotion company. He also approached music hands on, playing various instruments in several bands. But rather than trying to get his name in lights, Scott decided to help other people reach musical stardom. He worked for several labels including Mary Tyler Moore's MTM Records and MCA Records, and launched DreamWorks Nashville, which was part of Universal Music Group before the division shut down in 2005.

Scott started Big Machine Records in September of that year, and the company had its first number-one single, Jack Ingram's "Wherever You Are," eight months later. His early roster included Dusty Drake, Jack Ingram, Danielle Peck, Jimmy Wayne, and, of course, Taylor Swift. Though he jokes that when he told industry colleagues about his new 16-year-old sensation, "People would look at me cross-eyed. I would feel like they were deleting me from their BlackBerrys as I was telling them," he knew Taylor was a real talent. In 2006, he told *Billboard*, "I've had the good fortune of breaking everybody from Trisha Yearwood all the way up to Sugarland with big stops in between. This feels as big as any of them."

Since it opened its doors in 2005, Big Machine has expanded steadily, and in 2007, the CEO announced a new branch of Big Machine, Valory Music Group. The new division launched famed singer-songwriter Jewel's first country album, the debut album of *Billboard*'s "New Country Artist of 2009" Justin Moore, and represents Reba McEntire. In addition to Big Machine being distributed by Universal, Scott further re-established his connections with the major label in 2009 with a shared imprint, Republic Records Nashville, which represents acts such as The Band Perry and Sunny Sweeney. In 2012, Borchetta signed country superstar Tim McGraw, which helped Big Machine earn the title of number-one country label, according to *Billboard*. Through innovative partnerships and licensing deals, including the release of the *Nashville* TV series soundtrack, the little company that began in the mid-2000s has made big strides in a short time.

So how does Scott select who will become part of the Big Machine family? "I either fall in love with an artist's music or I don't," he explains. Good thing it was a love story with Taylor Swift's songs from day one.

Taylor with LeAnn Rimes, the singer who first got her interested in country music. Says Taylor: "Country music is the place to find reality in music, and reality in the stars who make that music. There's kindness and goodness and . . . honesty in the people I look up to, and knowing that makes me smile. I'm proud to sing country music, and that has never wavered."

of my sails, personally, if I had to sing words that other people wrote; that would have killed me." Scott Borchetta's faith in her and the independence he promised her were enough to seal the deal . . . even if his company didn't yet exist. "Obviously, creative control is the most important thing for me, or I wouldn't have left the biggest label in Nashville for a label that didn't have any furniture," joked Taylor.

With a star-in-the-making like Taylor signed on, Scott now had even more motivation to get the new label up and running. He knew he had found someone incredibly special: "I was just killed on sight. She's the full package, somebody who writes her own songs, and is so good at it, so smart; who sings, plays the guitar, looks as good as she looks, works that hard, is that engaging and so savvy. It's an extraordinary combination."

CHAPTER 3

A PLACE IN THIS WORLD

Scott Borchetta, Taylor, and Nathan Chapman, triumphant at the 2009 CMAs.
Only three years earlier Taylor was in the studio with Nathan and Scott recording
Taylor Swift.

With the support of Scott Borchetta and Big Machine Records, it was time for Taylor to start working on her first album. She entered the studio with Nathan Chapman, her demo producer, to record the tracks that would become her self-titled debut. Just like with Taylor's collaboration with Liz, she came to the studio with a definite idea of what her songs should sound like and Nathan's role as a producer was to translate those ideas into sonic perfection. She explained, "When I write a song I hear it completely produced in my head. I know exactly where I want the hook to be and I know what instruments I want to use. One of my favorite things to do is to sit around and obsess about how my music is going to sound. A lot of that goes on in the days following me writing a song. I will bring it into the studio with my producer Nathan, who I met when I was 14, and I will sing him the hook. We'll decide what we want to be playing on that. We've got it down to where we can understand each other before we even have to make much sense."

Over their many years of collaboration, Nathan has learned to trust Taylor's instincts: "Taylor knows just who she is. And she knows what she wants to say with the lyrics of her songs and with the music. She knows who she wants to be and where she fits in this big thing called the music business."

Though recording can be nerve-wracking for some new artists, Taylor wasn't intimidated by it, and saw it as a new extension of her dedication to music. She told GAC, "I love the recording process because I love singing, and it really gives me a chance to hone in on every single word — make it count, make it perfect." Ever the perfectionist, the process doesn't end for Taylor once her day in the recording booth does. She explained, "I leave the studio but I don't put it down. I don't stop listening and I don't stop tweaking and critiquing."

The tracks for the album were whittled down from a list of 40 songs to 11. When it came time to choose her first single, one song stood out for Scott Borchetta. Taylor had written it for a high school sweetheart, and she called it "When You Think Tim McGraw." Scott told *Dateline*, "She finished the song and I said, 'Do you realize what you just have written? Do you have any idea?' That was that moment of 'Oh my God.' And the grenade dropped in the still pond." The song's name was eventually shortened to "Tim McGraw," since that's how everyone referred to it. A quick session with Liz Rose at the piano perfected the song, Taylor recorded it, and her first single was released on June 19, 2006.

Over the next six months, "Tim McGraw" became almost as popular as its namesake: it hit number six on the Billboard Hot Country Songs chart and number 40 on the Hot 100 chart. Before the song hit the charts, Taylor got instant gratification when she was out for a drive and she heard her song requested on the radio for the first time. "I was, like, freaking out. I almost drove off the road," she told GAC.

When "Tim McGraw" was released, Taylor was finishing up her sophomore year at Hendersonville High. With her career taking off, a difficult decision had to be made: could she continue attending regular high school? She knew she wouldn't be able to dedicate herself 100% to her career if she had to keep a high-school timetable, so Taylor made the decision to homeschool. Abigail remembered, "She called me one night and we had to have the talk about [how] she's not coming back to school . . . we dealt with it, and we've actually gotten closer since." It was a hard transition for both girls. Said Abigail, "She had to do her own thing out there and miss everything that had been her life for the previous few years.

that his granddaughter was a big fan of Taylor's and that she was getting straight As. Scott thought this was just typical grandfatherly pride until the man added, "She wasn't getting straight As, but she heard Taylor Swift is getting straight As."

Taylor's new educational arrangement allowed her to study anytime, anywhere, which was especially useful as she embarked on a national radio tour. These kinds of tours can be exhausting with long hours, lots of travel, and endless interviews. She was "living in hotel rooms, sleeping in the backs of rental cars as my mom drove to three different cities in one day." But to Taylor, it was a great time. About all those interviews, she wrote, "I loooooved it because it's just talking to people. I could talk to a door." She brought her fiddle player and close pal, Emily Poe, and a guitar player, Todd, with her on the road, playing shows wherever they could.

Sometimes Taylor even went back to school — to play shows. Still self-conscious about her place in the high-school hierarchy, the experience could be nerve-wracking. "I remember when I first started doing high-school shows I was in the 10th grade," she told the *Washington Post*. "So it was a little more intimidating when I was 16 and first got on the road and started doing high-school shows and I'm like, 'Oh, there are seniors out there!'"

But she just immediately started doing so well . . . you just couldn't really think about anything else."

"My brother's always calling me the drop-out of the family," Taylor joked. "Drop-out" or not, Taylor continued her straight-A streak from her pre-homeschooling days. In fact, Taylor's scholastic success would become something her fans try to emulate. Scott Swift recounted an experience to the *Tennessean* about a man coming up to him and stating

Returning to high school meant remembering the little day-to-day experiences that she'd sacrificed for her career, but Taylor has no regrets about the path she chose. "You're always going to wonder about the road not taken, the dorm not taken, and the sorority not taken," she told CMT. "But if I wasn't doing this, I would've missed out on the best moments I've ever known and the most wonderful life that I still can't believe I get to live."

TAYLOR SWIFT

Taylor's self-titled debut album came out on October 24, 2006. It sold 39,000 copies in its first week, giving it the second-highest first-week sales for the year. (Taylor only fell behind friend Kellie Pickler, a defeat she's likely okay with!) It peaked at number one on the Billboard Top Country Albums chart and at number five on the Billboard 200, remaining on the chart for an incredibly long time. In fact, *Taylor Swift* set the record for the longest-charting album since Nielsen SoundScan started tracking sales in 1991, and after 157 weeks *Taylor Swift* passed Nickelback's *All the Right Reasons* to achieve the longest chart reign of the decade. The album went platinum a mere seven months after its release, and Taylor became the first solo female country artist to write or co-write every song on a platinum record.

At the time of its release Taylor's album didn't get as much media attention as her later albums would, but *Taylor Swift* was still well received. *AllMusic* reviewer Jeff Tamarkin noted that Taylor was equipped with "a fresh, still girlish voice, full of hope and naïveté, but it's also a confident and mature one," and added, "That Swift is a talent to be reckoned with is never in doubt." An About.com reviewer noted that Taylor "writes and sings with the passion and conviction of a veteran of country music." Later, the *New York Times* would hail the album as a "small masterpiece of pop-minded country."

Taylor followed up "Tim McGraw" with singles "Teardrops on My Guitar," "Our Song," "Picture to Burn," and "Should've Said No." All of them hit the top 10 on the Country Songs chart, and each song also found a spot on the Hot 100 list. Taylor had achieved the gold standard (or, more accurately, platinum standard) of music industry success — she had crossover appeal. Pop music listeners took to her songs almost as eagerly as country fans did.

Nashville producer and performer John

Rich explained, "You can hear great pop sensibilities in her writing as well as great storytelling, which is the trademark of old-school country song-crafting." Since her days belting out Dixie Chicks songs at karaoke contests, Taylor has known that her roots are in country music, and she's glad that her songs are drawing new fans to the genre. "I'd like to think that country music is where I live, country music is who I am, but I'm lucky enough to have other people listening who aren't necessarily core country music fans," said the singer. With her solid presence on the pop charts, Taylor has followed in the footsteps of the women she idolized as a child — LeAnn Rimes, Shania Twain, the Dixie Chicks, and Faith Hill. Despite Taylor's crossover success, Scott Borchetta still makes the country music crowd the label's first priority when it comes to all things Taylor Swift. "They're always going to get the singles first, always going to be first in line at the meet-and-greets," says the CEO. "We overthink everything. One thing we can't do is chase the moving target of pop radio." And Taylor wisely noted, "I'm not about to snub the people who brought me to the party."

Remarkably, she'd also conquered the demographic Nashville bigwigs had told her didn't exist: young, female country music fans. "So many girls come up and say to me, 'I have never listened to country music in my life. I didn't even know my town had a country music station. Then I got your record, and now I'm obsessed,'" related the singer. "That's the coolest compliment to me." Astounded by the ever-growing Taylor Nation comprised of young women, CMT exec Brian Philips reflected, "From the moment 'Tim McGraw' hit the channel, she began to amass an audience that traditional Nashville didn't know or didn't believe existed, and that is young women, specifically teens. It's as if Taylor has kind of willed herself into being." The path for Taylor's success was also paved by Carrie Underwood's breakthrough in 2005. When then-22-year-old Carrie won season four of *American Idol*, the Oklahoma native took her country-pop sound to the top of the charts with her debut album *Some Hearts*, which has since been certified seven-times platinum.

After Taylor's first album experienced similarly staggering success, Scott Borchetta had no difficulty forecasting a bright future for his young star: "My fear is that she'll conquer the world by the time she's 19. She'll get to the mountaintop and say, 'This is it?' Because she's just knocking down all of those goals that we didn't even have for the first album. . . . My job at this point is really to protect her and not burn her out." But with another album and tours already in sight, Taylor wasn't anywhere close to burning out. Instead, Taylor's success was spreading like wildfire.

CHAPTER 4

TAYLOR SWIFT
SWIFT NOTES

Many of Taylor's songs are about romantic relationships, but her very first and longest love affair is with words, and "Swift Notes" analyzes the songs on her albums just like Taylor dissects her past romances.

BEHIND THE MUSIC Details on Taylor's inspiration and writing process for the song.

BETWEEN THE LINES Taylor's an award-winning songwriter; find analysis of her lyrics here.

AUDIENCE OF ONE Taylor often writes her songs with a very specific audience in mind: "When I sit down and write a song the only person that I'm thinking about in that room is the person that I'm writing the song about and what I want them to know and what I wish I could tell them to their face, but I'm going to say it in a song instead." Wonder if she's singing about someone in particular? Find out in this section.

FUN FACTS These are extra tidbits about the song and Taylor.

DIARY DECODER Taylor encodes a secret message into the lyrics in her album booklets; this section solves the puzzles and discusses why Taylor chose that particular message.

CHARTING SUCCESS Taylor's been smashing sales records since her debut. Find out how her singles did and info on awards she's won.

1. "TIM MCGRAW"

BEHIND THE MUSIC Taylor wrote this song during math class in a mere 15 minutes, polished it after school, added piano, and finished it up with Liz!

BETWEEN THE LINES Despite the fact that his name is mentioned six times, this wistful ballad isn't about the famous country singer, but rather uses Tim McGraw as a sort of musical memento. The song is like a letter to her departed boyfriend, and an actual letter is mentioned in the song's second verse. "Tim McGraw" is about a relationship that ended when the guy left for college ("September was a month of tears" because that's when he went away). The lyrics also reveal what would become part of Taylor's signature style: alternating between a "little black dress" and her more casual "old faded blue jeans."

AUDIENCE OF ONE Taylor went out with the boy this song's about (rumored to be Brandon Borello) when she was a freshman and he was a senior. Though they may be broken up, he's still a Taylor Swift fan: "He bought the album and said he really loved it, which is sweet," said Taylor. "His current girlfriend isn't too pleased with it, though." And what did Tim McGraw himself have to say about it? "It was awesome, except that I didn't know if I should take it as a compliment or if I should feel old," said the country star. "But the more I hear it . . . I start taking it as a compliment."

FUN FACTS Since releasing "Tim McGraw," Taylor's become great friends with Tim and his wife, Faith Hill.

Taylor introduces herself to Tim McGraw at the ACM Awards on May 15, 2007.

DIARY DECODER The secret message is "Can't Tell Me Nothin'," the Tim McGraw song (from *Live Like You Were Dying*) Taylor had in mind while writing her song.

CHARTING SUCCESS Taylor's first single peaked at number six on the Billboard Country Songs chart, and number 40 on the Hot 100. "Tim McGraw" was certified gold on May 3, 2007, and later went platinum. Its video won the Breakthrough Video of the Year award at the 2007 CMT Music Awards. Taylor was shocked by its success, saying, "It never really occurred to me that that song would be so relatable."

2. "PICTURE TO BURN"

BEHIND THE MUSIC One day Taylor arrived at

her after-school job at Sony in a rage about a boy. She started playing her guitar and venting, "I hate his stupid truck that he doesn't let me drive. He's such a redneck! Oh my God!" Some of those very words found their way into the song's chorus.

BETWEEN THE LINES Taylor told the *Washington Post*, "It's about a guy I liked who didn't like me back, and I got really mad, you know?" The two never officially dated because, Taylor explained, "It really bothered me that he was so cocky and that's where that song came from."

AUDIENCE OF ONE Taylor's not sure if he knows about this song, but if he does, hopefully he's learned a thing or two and now lets his girlfriend drive his pickup truck.

FUN FACTS When she was younger, one of Taylor's favorite karaoke songs was the Dixie Chicks' "Goodbye Earl," a song with a similar message — don't get mad, get even. You'll hear a slightly different version of this song on the radio — the line "That's fine, I'll tell mine that you're gay" is replaced with "That's fine, you won't mind if I say," since Taylor never meant to offend anyone.

DIARY DECODER "Date nice boys" — wise advice, indeed.

CHARTING SUCCESS The fourth single from Taylor's first album, "Picture to Burn" hit number three on the Billboard Country Songs chart and number 28 on the Hot 100. Looks like pop music fans like their country songs with a little fire in them! "Picture to Burn" was also included on the 2008 compilation of country hits *Now That's What I Call Country*. The song was certified gold on June 11, 2008.

3. "TEARDROPS ON MY GUITAR"

BEHIND THE MUSIC Taylor wasn't actually crying over her guitar when the idea for this sad song came to her; she was on her way home from school.

BETWEEN THE LINES "Teardrops on My Guitar" is about Taylor's crush on her friend Drew Hardwick, who liked to talk to Taylor about his girlfriend all the time. Taylor explained to *Seventeen*, "I had it bad for him. And I just kept thinking, 'Why am I so invisible to him? Why does he have to have a girlfriend?' I never told him that I liked him, but I did write a song with his name on it." Taylor further explored this feeling of "girl-next-door-itis," as she calls it, in "You Belong with Me." Teardrops on her guitar is a great image of Taylor working through the tough stuff with music.

AUDIENCE OF ONE Two years after the song came out, Taylor was heading to a hockey game with Kellie Pickler and Carrie Underwood when she got quite a surprise: "[Drew] was standing there in my driveway. I haven't talked to this guy in two years. I was like, 'Um, hi?' It would have been really cool and poetic if he had turned up at my house right after my album came out. But it was two years later. A couple of things had happened in my life since then. I was like, 'It's really great to see you. But you're a little late.'"

FUN FACTS The striking cover image of this single made a second appearance on Taylor's 2007 Christmas album, *Songs of the Season*.

DIARY DECODER This message reads, "He will never know" but, of course, after Drew showed up on her driveway, Taylor knows he does.

CHARTING SUCCESS "Teardrops" rose to number two on the Billboard Country Songs chart,

and number 13 on the Hot 100. It also hit the top 10 on the Pop Songs, Adult Pop Songs, and Adult Contemporary lists. "Teardrops on My Guitar" won Song of the Year at the 2008 BMI Country Awards for getting the most airtime of any country song that year. The song was certified gold in 2007 and hit double platinum in 2009.

4. "A PLACE IN THIS WORLD"

BEHIND THE MUSIC Inspiration for this song struck Taylor as she walked the streets of Nashville shortly after moving there. She told GAC, "I was just sort of looking around at all these big buildings and these important people and wondering how I was going to fit in."

BETWEEN THE LINES Taylor wrote this song about trying to make it in Nashville, but the song relates to any major life change, big risk, or just trying to figure out where we fit in. As Taylor has shown her fans, pursuing goals despite your trepidation can really pay off!

AUDIENCE OF ONE A lot of her songs are written for other people, but this one is really written for Taylor, or for the Taylor she wanted to be. Looking back, Taylor said, "I feel like I finally figured it out."

FUN FACTS "A Place in This World" is also the name of the GAC *Shortcuts* special on Taylor, included on the deluxe edition of *Taylor Swift*.

DIARY DECODER "I found it" — great reassurance that it's worth taking a leap of faith if you're "ready to fly."

5. "COLD AS YOU"

BEHIND THE MUSIC "Cold as You" emerged from a songwriting session with Liz, and although

Taylor thinks it contains "some of the best lyrics I've ever written in my life," she didn't come up with the hook until halfway through the songwriting process. She told *Rolling Stone*, "I love a line in a song where afterward you're just like *burn*."

BETWEEN THE LINES In another track about unrequited love, Taylor explores a relationship with someone who doesn't appreciate her. "It's about that moment where you realize someone isn't at all who you thought they were, and that you've been trying to make excuses for someone who doesn't deserve them. And that some people are just never going to love you," explained the songwriter.

AUDIENCE OF ONE Taylor chose not to single out the guy with the icy heart, but the folks back in her hometown like to speculate. "You go out into this big world, and you go back and it's still a small town and they still gossip about it. I think it's one of everybody's favorite things to talk about — who my songs are written about," said Taylor. "There are definitely a few more people who think that I've written songs about them than there actually are."

DIARY DECODER More great advice: "Time to let go." Was the message for Taylor herself?

6. "THE OUTSIDE"

BEHIND THE MUSIC This is one of the very first songs Taylor wrote, when she was 12 and wasn't fitting in at school.

BETWEEN THE LINES Most people feel like an outsider at some point, and for Taylor that time was in middle school. She confided to *Entertainment Weekly*, "I wrote that about the scariest feeling I've ever felt: going to school,

walking down the hall, looking at all those faces, and not knowing who you're gonna talk to that day. People always ask, 'How did you have the courage to walk up to record labels when you were 12 or 13?' It's because I could never feel the kind of rejection in the music industry that I felt in middle school." Being on the outside did have its benefits: it fueled Taylor's songwriting and encouraged her to embrace what made her different. Taylor writes, "I tried to take the road less traveled by," a reference to the famous Robert Frost poem, "The Road Not Taken," in which he writes, "I took the one less traveled by, / And

TAYLOR SWIFT: DELUXE EDITION

On November 6, 2007, fans who were crying out for more Taylor were rewarded with the release of a deluxe edition of *Taylor Swift*. The album contained three previously unreleased songs that Taylor calls "some of my favorites" from her demo-making days at age 14 and 15, plus a recording of Taylor's first phone call with Tim McGraw. The first new song, "I'm Only Me When I'm with You," talks about finding a person who loves you for who you are. It's a philosophy that Taylor embraces 100%. She told *Seventeen*, "The guy I'm looking for is the guy I can be me around, not a version of me I think he'd like." Taylor released a video for this song, which used home movie footage, and tided fans over until the "Picture to Burn" video came out. She noted, "I think it's the only video CMT has probably ever played that cost, like, five dollars to make." The second tune, "Invisible," revisits the themes of "Teardrops on My Guitar." The third new track, "A Perfectly Good Heart," pleads with an unnamed heartbreaker as Taylor tries to figure out how to make her heart whole again. The CD came with a DVD featuring Taylor's previously released videos, behind-the-scenes featurettes, performance footage, her GAC *Shortcuts* series "A Place in This World," and a special home video compiled by the singer herself.

that has made all the difference." Looks like it did for Taylor too.

AUDIENCE OF ONE This is a song for all the people who made Taylor feel excluded. Did they get the message? Hopefully. One thing's for sure: many of the mean girls who made her feel so alone had a change in attitude when Taylor hit the big time. Taylor told *Teen Vogue*, "I played a hometown show about a year into my career, and they showed up wearing my T-shirts and asking me to sign their CDs. It was bittersweet, because it made me realize that they didn't remember being mean to me and that I needed to forget about it too. And really, if I hadn't come home from school miserable every day, maybe I wouldn't have been so motivated to write songs. I should probably be thanking them!"

(NOT SO) FUN FACTS A study found that almost 30% of kids and teens in the U.S. are involved in bullying (that's over 5.7 million people!). For more information about bullying and support groups, go to bullying.org.

DIARY DECODER This secret message reads, "You are not alone." Even though being excluded can make you feel completely alone, people everywhere are going through the same thing. So at the very least, it's some comfort to know that you're never alone in feeling alone.

CHARTING SUCCESS This song was not a single, but it was Taylor's first-ever release, appearing on *Chicks with Attitude* in 2004.

7. "TIED TOGETHER WITH A SMILE"

BEHIND THE MUSIC Taylor wrote this song after finding out a friend was bulimic. It was a revelation that the songwriter describes as "one of those moments when your heart kinda stops." And though Taylor had written about painful things before, she noted, "This one was tough to write, because I wasn't just telling some sad story. This was real."

BETWEEN THE LINES "Tied Together with a Smile" explores the notion that people aren't always what they seem, that the most outwardly confident person could actually be the most vulnerable. The friend who Taylor wrote it about was a pageant queen, "the golden one" she references in the song. "Girls want to be her and guys want to be with her," said Taylor. Though "The Outside" explains how hard it can be to be excluded from the in-crowd, "Tied Together with a Smile" shows that being popular has its own set of challenges. "This song is basically about the girls I know, and the difficult things I saw them go through," explained Taylor. "I've never seen this song as a lecture. It's really about how no matter what my friends go through, I'm always going to love them."

AUDIENCE OF ONE This is a sad story with a happy ending — Taylor's friend got help and is healthy once again.

(NOT SO) FUN FACTS The National Institute for Mental Health found that one in five women struggle with some kind of eating disorder. Luckily there are lots of great organizations that can help. In the U.S., the National Eating Disorders Association is a great source of information and also provides a referral service (www.nationaleatingdisorders.org; 1-800-931-2237). In Canada, the National Eating Disorder Information Centre provides similar services (www.nedic.ca; 1-866-NEDIC-20).

DIARY DECODER People with eating disorders struggle with self-image and self-worth; "You are loved" is one of the most important messages they can get.

8. "STAY BEAUTIFUL"

BEHIND THE MUSIC Taylor's songs may make it seem like she's had a lot of boyfriends, but she didn't date all the boys she's singing about. In "Stay Beautiful," the songwriter merely admired her crush from afar. She explained, "This song is about a guy I thought was cute, and never really talked to much. But something about him inspired this song, just watching him."

BETWEEN THE LINES "Stay Beautiful" is a reminder of how perfect things appear from a distance. With "Stay Beautiful" following "Tied Together with a Smile" it seems like the lyrics "You're beautiful / Every little piece love, don't you know / You're really gonna be someone, ask anyone" are also wonderful reassurance for those, like Taylor's friend, who can't see that for themselves.

AUDIENCE OF ONE This song's for Cory, and there's no doubt he'd be flattered to hear it!

FUN FACTS Taylor has another song about admiring someone from afar on *Fearless: Platinum Edition*, but in "SuperStar" that person is untouchable because he's a celeb.

DIARY DECODER Taylor's not always serious, and the playful message "Shake N Bake" is a bit of a mystery. Maybe she liked Cory as much as this savory dinner staple?

9. "SHOULD'VE SAID NO"

BEHIND THE MUSIC Taylor penned this raging tune at the studio right after confronting a boyfriend who was cheating on her. She wrote it just in time to squeeze it onto the album at the last minute. She admitted on her blog, "I wrote it about 20 minutes before we recorded it. It just kind of fell out of my mouth and now it is in my CD player."

BETWEEN THE LINES "Should've Said No" is the second angry anthem on the album, but has a different message than "Picture to Burn." In this case the focus falls more on bad decision-making than on the guy. Taylor explained, "Just being a human being, I've realized that before every big problem you create for yourself, before every huge mess you have to clean up, there was a crucial moment where you could've just said no." Straight-as-an-arrow Taylor doesn't just preach it; she lives it and is often in the media spotlight for being a performer who *hasn't* gone off the rails. Taylor credits her folks for her good decision-making, saying, "My parents have instilled a great level of trust in me and I think that's a huge, huge part of who I am. I can tell my mom everything, and I do. Before I make decisions, I always think, 'What is my mom going to think if I tell her this? Is my mom going to be really upset if she finds out that I did this?' Usually I decide, 'No, I'm not going to go through with this.'"

AUDIENCE OF ONE Thanks to the secret message, it's clear this song's for Sam, and though he hasn't commented about the public shaming, Taylor wasn't done with him after her first album. Before the release of *Fearless*, Taylor told *Girls' Life*: "I wrote a few more songs on this upcoming record about him just because, you know, I wasn't done being mad about it. I know he's on the edge of his seat waiting."

FUN FACTS Sam should have followed Taylor's lead — she says "no" eight times in this song.

DIARY DECODER This message is a pointed finger: "Sam Sam Sam Sam Sam."

CHARTING SUCCESS "Should've Said No" was Taylor's second number one on the Billboard Country Songs chart, and hit number 33 on the Hot 100. The song was certified gold on September 3, 2008, and platinum on October 12, 2009.

10. "MARY'S SONG (OH MY MY MY)"

BEHIND THE MUSIC Taylor wrote this song after the couple next door came over for dinner and told the Swift family about how they met as children and later fell in love.

BETWEEN THE LINES After the anger in "Should've Said No," it's nice to follow with a song where a romance worked out. "Mary's Song" follows the couple as they go from being playmates to the beginning of their romance to the proposal and wedding. It's a song brimming with love and hope, and Taylor noted, "I thought it was so sweet, because you can go to the grocery store and read the tabloids, and see who's breaking up and cheating on each other (or just listen to some of my songs, haha). But it was really comforting to know that all I had to do was go home and look next door to see a perfect example of forever."

AUDIENCE OF ONE This song is for Mary and her husband; maybe one day Taylor will write a new verse about their continued happiness.

Taylor performs "Should've Said No" at the 2008 ACM Awards.

FUN FACTS Taylor and Liz share their co-writing credit on this song with Brian Dean Maher, a Nashville songwriter.

DIARY DECODER This romantic tune has an appropriately hopeful message: "Sometimes love is forever."

11. "OUR SONG"

BEHIND THE MUSIC In ninth grade, Taylor realized she and her boyfriend didn't have a song. Inspiration struck while she was sitting in her living room; she "sat down one day with my guitar and got in a groove" and wrote him a song, one that she would perform in front of all of Hendersonville High at the talent show.

BETWEEN THE LINES Taylor chose to end the album on a high note with this infectious tune about all the ordinary things that can be part of a great love. Right at the end of the chorus, Taylor slyly says, "Play it again" in hopes that listeners would give her record another spin!

AUDIENCE OF ONE With this final song, Taylor's

SONGS OF THE SEASON:
THE TAYLOR SWIFT HOLIDAY COLLECTION

A major celebration in the Swift home, Christmas is Taylor's favorite holiday. She wrote on her blog, "I love everything about this time of year, but mostly the way that people find ways to be with the ones they love." With her love of all things Christmas, it was a natural choice for her to release a holiday album. On October 14, 2007, Big Machine released the limited-edition album exclusively in Target and online. Despite these restrictions, the album still climbed to number 14 on the Billboard Top Country Albums chart and to number 20 on the Hot 200.

Taylor covered four Christmas classics: "White Christmas" (originally performed by Bing Crosby), "Santa Baby" (originally performed by Eartha Kitt, and later by Madonna), "Last Christmas" (originally performed by Wham!), and the traditional "Silent Night." Never one to only sing other people's compositions, Taylor added a couple of original songs that offered a twist on the usual seasonal fare. She insisted, "There's got to be something really original and different about it." The heartbreaking "Christmases When You Were Mine" (co-written with Liz Rose and producer Nathan Chapman) is about remembering love from Christmases past, and "Christmas Must Be Something More" encouraged people to see past the gifts to the sacred spirit of the season.

Though the album was supposed to be a one-time release, Taylor Swift fans who still hope to see this album under the tree are in luck; it was re-released in October 2009.

first high-school romance is the focus of the first and last tracks on the album. And though she is no longer in touch with that boyfriend, he must be just as pleased with the album as when he was in the audience at the talent show. FUN FACTS This became Taylor's third single because it was a fan favorite in concert. Don't confuse this song with another popular ballad, Elton John's "Your Song," which is also about writing a song for a loved one. DIARY DECODER The album's last secret message, "Live in love," applies not just to "Our Song," but Taylor Swift as a whole. The album

features everything from first love to fury, and these highs and lows are part of living life to the fullest. And if life and love are just the way Taylor sings it, who would want to miss a moment? CHARTING SUCCESS "Our Song" was Taylor's first number one, and she refused to give up her spot for six weeks! That six-week stay at the top of the Country Songs chart ties her with one of her heroes, Faith Hill, and her song "Breathe," and both women are topped only by the reign of Connie Smith's 1964 song "Once a Day." "Our Song" also made Taylor the youngest person to write a number-one single on her own. The song also hit number 16 on the Hot 100 and number 24 on the Pop 100, continuing Taylor's crossover success that began with "Teardrops on My Guitar." "Our Song" won Video of the Year at the 2008 CMT Music Awards. The "Our Song" single has earned double platinum certification.

CHAPTER 5

LEARNING FROM LEGENDS

In April 2007, Taylor returned to Pennsylvania to play the Sovereign Performing Arts Center in Reading.

"I just went to a show by a future superstar," starts an About.com review of a performance Taylor gave on May 30, 2007, at the Gold Country Casino. With a hot new album on their hands, Big Machine was trying to give Taylor all the exposure she could get, and Taylor played some of her first headlining shows. Her career was picking up speed, and nowhere was that more evident than when she returned to her hometown to play a concert at the Sovereign Performing Arts Center in Reading, Pennsylvania. It was a place where

Taylor had once been in the audience, gazing at performers like Melissa Etheridge from afar. Now, just a few years later, she was center stage, telling the crowd about her journey by paraphrasing one of her favorite songs, Eminem's "Lose Yourself." "See, when I left three years ago," she told the crowd, "I had one shot, one opportunity to seize everything I ever wanted. Y'all think I did alright?"

Though she continued to do some headlining gigs where she could, Taylor racked up most of her experience touring as an opener

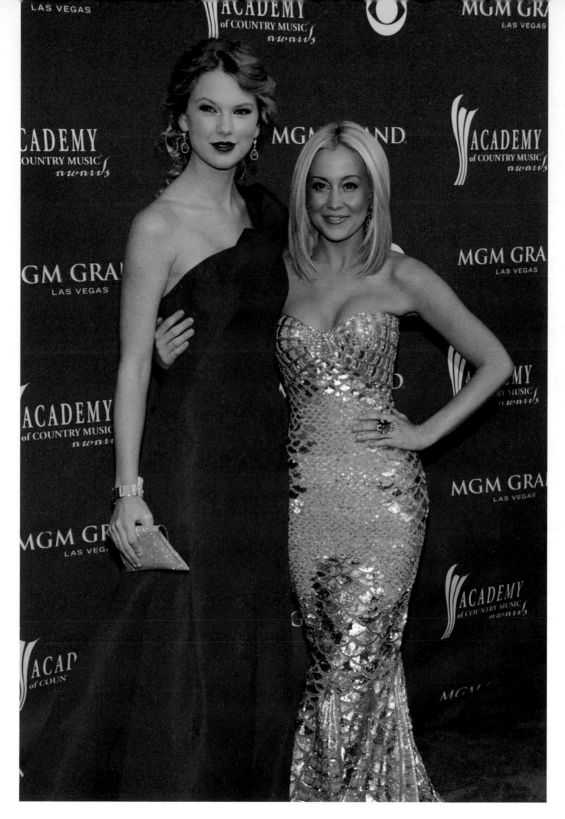

Said Taylor of Kellie Pickler: "She's like a sister. People say we're such opposites, but that's what makes us such good friends. She's incredibly blunt. I love that about her. If some guy has said or done something to me she doesn't like, she'll grab my cell phone and say, 'I'm deleting his number.'" The two co-wrote Kellie's first top 10 hit "Best Days of Your Life," with Taylor singing on the track and appearing in its video.

By 2009, Taylor was not just opening for country legends, she was sharing the stage with them. Pictured here with Rascal Flatts, Carrie Underwood, Brooks & Dunn, and Sugarland at the ACMs on April 5.

for country greats. In October 2006, she hit the road with Rascal Flatts, the three-man country act known for hits such as "What Hurts the Most," "Bless the Broken Road," and a cover of Tom Cochrane's "Life Is a Highway," which was on the soundtrack to Pixar's *Cars*. Finding out she'd be part of her first major tour, Taylor wrote, "I'm SO excited and I can't even express to you how loud I screamed when I found out." She played nine acoustic shows with the group, and Taylor really meshed with the trio, and she toured again with them two years later. During her 2008 tour with the band, she wrote on her blog, "The Rascal Flatts tour is SO much fun. I'm loving it so much, and the guys are so cool. They'll just walk onto my bus and say hi. It's so cool that the guys from Rascal Flatts are so down to earth." Though she dreamed of having a tour to call her own, Taylor wisely realized that she could learn a lot from touring with industry pros. She explained, "I didn't mind opening for Rascal Flatts because you learn something from every single tour you go on, and I felt I had more to learn."

The next stop on Taylor's tour of country star tours was a gig opening for the King of Country himself, George Strait, from January to March 2007. On her blog, Taylor gushed, "I'm pretty much a George Strait superfan, so this is going to be SO much fun." Sure enough, playing with the legendary country icon was thrilling for the young star. Taylor wrote, "I'm pretty sure the highlight of my night last night (the first show of the tour, in Lafayette, LA) was that . . . George Strait SAID MY NAME . . . [We] were watching George's show . . . and all of a sudden he says, 'I'm very happy to have the talented Miss Taylor Swift out here with us.' YESSSSS. It was pretty awesome, sort of a life changing moment."

But her encounters with country music's finest didn't end there — Taylor's next tour would be with country rocker Brad Paisley on his 2007 Bonfires & Amplifiers tour. Brad told *Blender*, "I was looking at a lot of artists to come out on tour with us, but as soon as I downloaded her album, I knew we had to have her. I was floored by the songwriting. I love the fact that she doesn't pretend to be 30 years old in her songs. She has a very genuine voice." Taylor knew she had a lot to learn from Brad, and noted, "I try to pick his brain and learn as much as I can from him."

Also on the Bonfires & Amplifiers tour were labelmate Jack Ingram and pal Kellie Pickler. The three injected a lot of energy and more than a little silliness into the tour, like on the night they decided to prank the headliner. Taylor ordered tick costumes for her and

If you missed Taylor when she was an opening act, here's an example of her set list from an April 10, 2008, show in Sacramento, CA.

- "I'm Only Me When I'm with You"
- "Our Song"
- "Teardrops on My Guitar"
- "Should've Said No"
- "Tim McGraw"
- "Picture to Burn"

Kellie, and Jack put together an exterminator suit. When Brad started playing his new song "Ticks," Kellie and Taylor emerged in costume, and danced around Brad onstage. Out came Exterminator Ingram who pretended to spray them with insecticide then the bugs faked an elaborate death. Writing about it on her MySpace, Taylor recalled, "I was laughing so hard I could barely breathe. Then I was laying there on the stage playing dead, and looked up at Brad, and he looked down at me and said, 'Nice work.'" Guess he was a little bit "bugged." Not to worry, Brad was a prankster himself, and forced Jack Ingram into a cage and made him perform from there!

While Brad was on a break from touring, Taylor opened shows for another country great, Kenny Chesney. Once again, the person she idolized did not disappoint in real life. "Opening up for Kenny Chesney is one of the coolest things I've ever done," said Taylor. "His tour has this laidback vibe to it, and everyone's so cool to work with. And Kenny Chesney is so completely nice. Genuinely nice."

The rising star learned something from all of her mentors on tour, summing up for *USA Weekend*, "Kenny is up at the crack of dawn, walking around the venue, getting to know everyone from the sound-check guys to the people who sell the souvenirs to the fans. Then Rascal Flatts stages this big production with all the flash. And George Strait? It's all about the music with him. He pays so much attention to building up the song with the arrangements and the band and his singing."

In the summer of 2007, the rising star hit another major career milestone when she toured with two people who inspired her love for country music in the first place — Tim McGraw and Faith Hill. Taylor played a four-song acoustic set before the dynamite duo performed on their Soul2Soul II tour. Getting to know the artists she idolized could have been a real letdown, but Taylor found the couple to be as wonderful as she'd always imagined them. Of Faith she wrote, "As beautiful as she is, she is THAT nice."

Even when Taylor only played a handful of songs as an opening act, reviewers took note. When she opened for Rascal Flatts in early 2008, one reviewer remarked, "If Swift's performance last night was any indication of what the future has to bring, surely there will be many more Grammy nominations, and eventually wins for the young songstress." What an accurate prediction!

Though Taylor confessed, "I've always wanted to be so busy I couldn't stand it," she still managed to get the occasional break from touring, and would head back to Hendersonville. On one such break, she wrote, "I just got back from a five show run on the road. Now I'm sitting in my kitchen . . . on the counter. Eating cool whip. And trying to think of things to do with my free time. Other than talking to my cat and making playlists of sad songs." Though it was nice to be reunited with her entire family, the overachiever didn't like to sit still too long — there were charts to climb, airwaves to conquer, and crowds to entertain. She admitted to *Bliss*, "I do love coming home, but after about a day I usually end up calling my record label and bugging them for something to do."

CHAPTER 6

GOLDEN GIRL

As an opener for major country music acts, Taylor spent a lot of her time playing second fiddle to the legendary stars she toured with. But as her first awards season approached in 2007, Taylor was about to prove that she had the chops to be the main event.

With more and more people listening to Taylor's music on MySpace or requesting her songs on the radio, the Taylor Nation of devoted fans was growing every day. And it couldn't have been any clearer than on April 16, 2007, when Taylor took home the fan-voted CMT Music Award in the Breakthrough Video category for "Tim McGraw." Taylor's first award was a sign of the strength of her fans' dedication, which would help raise Taylor to the top of the music industry, and she knew it, offering a thank-you on her blog to all the fans who helped make her dreams come true: "I've always been the girl watching the award shows from the stands or from my couch, wishing like crazy that someday if I worked hard enough and things really came together, that could be me. You did that for me." And as a special thank-you, she brought her award ("The Buckle") with her on the Brad Paisley tour, so fans could see the award they helped her win.

Fans are one thing, but getting industry respect is another. Six months after her CMT Music Award, it became abundantly clear that country music's finest were behind Taylor too. At the 2007 Country Music Association (CMA) Awards on November 7, Taylor won the prestigious Horizon Award, which goes to the most promising new artist of the year. As the previous year's winner Carrie Underwood explained as she presented it, "This is an award that means you have *truly* arrived in country music." Past winners include Garth Brooks, Keith Urban, Brad Paisley, LeAnn Rimes, and the Dixie Chicks. In her acceptance speech, Taylor was sure to thank the fans, tearfully insisting, "You have changed my life!" before finishing, "This is definitely the highlight of my senior year," a comment that got chuckles from the crowd. On her blog, Taylor shared what was going through her mind in this fairytale moment: "I remember it all in slow motion . . . I'm running up the stairs in a ball gown and heels. My mom and dad are crying. Everyone at my record label is screaming. My family and everyone I love is watching from their living rooms. I'm crying on national television, and thinking about [the fans]." She concluded, "And thank you for convincing me that fairytale endings . . . Well, they happen sometimes."

FEARLESS SONGBIRD

When Taylor sat down in December 2007 to start planning her sophomore album, she knew she had a tough act to follow — her self-titled debut had just been certified double platinum. "Pressure is one of my favorite things in the world," Taylor told the *Tennessean*. "When I heard before my second album, 'Is she going to experience a sophomore slump?' it made me more motivated to make sure that didn't happen. 'Is she going to keep this fan base?' 'Is this thing going to run off the tracks?' Those things motivate me. My gut instinct has worked so far, and I'm not going to mess with that."

One of the positive side effects of her

BEAUTIFUL EYES

The wait between Taylor's first and second albums was a long one for her dedicated fans. So on July 15, 2008, Taylor released *Beautiful Eyes*, six songs packaged with a DVD. The EP, which would only be available online and at Walmart, had two songs which Taylor wrote when she was 13 ("Beautiful Eyes" and "I Heart ?") as well as alternate versions of "Should've Said No," "Teardrops on My Guitar," "Picture to Burn," and "I'm Only Me When I'm with You" (which was on the deluxe edition of *Taylor Swift*). The DVD had all of Taylor's videos, her ACM performance of "Should've Said No," and a special homemade video for "Beautiful Eyes" with footage from her 18th birthday party. "I've gotten so many emails from people asking for new songs, and I thought this might tide them over till the new album comes out in the fall," Taylor explained on her MySpace blog. This limited-run album still managed to top the Billboard Country chart just two weeks after its release, with the number two spot going to *Taylor Swift*. Overwhelmed by her one-two domination of the charts, the singer blogged, "I can't believe it. My record label is freaking out because apparently the last time this happened was in 1997??" The person who accomplished that in 1997? None other than Taylor's first inspiration, LeAnn Rimes.

tremendous success is that the certified country star had proven she was a girl who knew what she was doing, and she was given even more creative control on her second record. Nathan Chapman, who worked on her first record, was back in the studio to produce, but this time Taylor officially stepped up as co-producer. A lucky 13 tracks would make the cut and appear on *Fearless*, including the last-minute addition "Forever & Always."

Beyond supervising, writing, and recording the music, Taylor was heavily involved in the album design as well. On her MySpace, Taylor wrote, "I'm completely going crazy thinking of ideas for the album photo shoots and the CD booklet and all of that stuff. I'm consumed and obsessed and so excited that I get to make a second record. Hey, I'm still in awe of the fact that I got to make the first one." She and her label found the right photographer, Nashville's Joseph Anthony Baker, and Taylor played the album for him to see which songs spoke to him. What resulted was a gorgeous array of photographs of Taylor inspired by the songs. "We shot photos based on the energy of that song," explained the singer-temporarily-turned-model. And what about the album cover image of Taylor's face framed by a halo of windswept golden curls? "The photographer put the wind machine on, like, hurricane mode," said Taylor. "That's how we got the picture." Taylor oversaw every aspect of the album down to the smallest details, once again encoding secret messages in her lyrics.

Taylor kept her fans up to date on the album's progress, writing, "This next record is on my mind 24/7, all the time. It never stops. I'm always either listening to a new mix of a song or scanning through pictures to make sure we've chosen the right ones, or wondering which songs you guys are going to like the best. I'm just so obsessed with it right now, all the planning."

The album would be called *Fearless*, a name that Taylor explained in the liner notes: "FEARLESS is not the absence of fear. It's not being completely unafraid. To me, FEARLESS is having fears. FEARLESS is having doubts. Lots of them. To me, FEARLESS is living in spite of those things that scare you to death."

Despite her success, country music's golden girl isn't without her own fears. She explained to *Girls' Life*, "I think things on the record that

are talked about have a very fearless quality to them. It's not about me being this fearless person because I'm afraid of everything, you know? I'm afraid of finding the most perfect love and losing it. I'm afraid of regretting things. I'm afraid of my career becoming mediocre and not being able to excite people anymore. I'm afraid of running out of things to write about. But I think there's something fearless about jumping, even when you're really scared of where you might land."

Taylor made that leap on November 11, 2008, with the release of *Fearless*, launching it on *Good Morning America*, just as she had with her first record. In its debut week, *Fearless* hit number one on both the Billboard 200 and the Top Country Albums charts. It would go on to spend eight weeks at number one, making it the first female country album to do so. Her sophomore album sold 217,000 copies on its first day alone, and after only one week in stores it was over halfway to platinum certification, with 592,000 copies sold. One of those copies was Taylor's; she stopped in at the Hendersonville Walmart at midnight to buy one the minute it was released. At that moment Taylor still had butterflies. She admitted, "The night before it came out, I remember staying up all night and thinking, 'Is anyone going to buy it at all?' You always have those last-minute jitters." But the overwhelming support from her fans was the best reassurance Taylor could have ever hoped for. "I've never been more proud of anything in my life . . . I wrote every song on it. I co-produced it. So to have people go out and actually buy it? It's wonderful," she told *Newsday*.

"I think any time you've had this kind of success it starts to get weighty," Scott Borchetta told the *LA Times*. "But she's delivered a brilliant record." For the most part, reviewers agreed. *Rolling Stone* (which honored her with a cover story in March 2009) praised, "Swift is a songwriting savant with an intuitive gift

for verse-chorus-bridge architecture that, in singles like the surging 'Fifteen,' calls to mind Swedish pop gods Dr. Luke and Max Martin. If she ever tires of stardom, she could retire to Sweden and make a fine living churning out hits for Kelly Clarkson and Katy Perry." The reviewer added, "Her music mixes an almost impersonal professionalism — it's so rigorously crafted it sounds like it has been scientifically engineered in a hit factory — with confessions that are squirmingly intimate and true." *Blender* gave it four stars out of five, with the reviewer noting, "Swift has the personality and poise to make these songs hit as hard as gems like 'Tim McGraw' and 'Our Song' from her smash debut, and, once again, she wrote or co-wrote them all." More praise came from *AllMusic*, which concluded, "Swift's gentle touch is as enduring as her song-craft, and this musical maturity may not jibe with her age, but it does help make *Fearless* one of the best mainstream pop albums of 2008."

CHAPTER 7

FEARLESS
SWIFT NOTES

1. "FEARLESS"

BEHIND THE MUSIC The idea for this song came to Taylor while she was touring. She didn't have a boyfriend and she started thinking about her ideal first date. She explained, "I think sometimes when you're writing love songs, you don't write them about what you're going through at the moment, you write about what you wish you had. So this song is about the best first date I haven't had yet."

BETWEEN THE LINES Taylor described "Fearless" as "about an incredible first date when all your walls are coming down and you are fearlessly jumping into love." And what's Taylor's idea of a great first date? She told *Girls' Life*, "I live on a lake, so it's really fun to go out on the boat, and then hang out all night and just talk. It wouldn't have to be anything fancy or anything like that, but just being with a person who gets you. It's kind of funny because you don't ever have a lot of opportunities like that to be home and to go on a date in your hometown, but that's exactly what I would do." Standing in the rain had been associated with the stormy anger of her "Should've Said No" performance at the 2008 ACM Awards, but on the title track of her second album, it's a sign of reckless abandon, of overcoming trepidation for something worthwhile.

AUDIENCE OF ONE Since this one isn't based on a real-life date, it's not for a specific lucky guy, but the message to be fearless is great advice for everyone.

FUN FACTS Taylor and Liz share co-writing credits for "Fearless" with Hillary Lindsey, who's penned songs for Bon Jovi, Miley Cyrus, and Martina McBride, but is best known for her work with Carrie Underwood, including the Grammy-winning single "Jesus, Take the Wheel." Colbie Caillat, Taylor's collaborator on "Breathe," also has a song called "Fearless" on her 2009 album, *Breakthrough*. Colbie's is about the end of a relationship and having the courage to carry on after heartbreak.

DIARY DECODER This optimistic song's message for a future sweetheart says, "I loved you before I met you."

CHARTING SUCCESS Before her later hits landed higher spots, "Fearless," her fifth single from *Fearless*, was Taylor's highest chart debut on the Billboard Hot 100, sitting at number nine in its first week. "Fearless" also peaked at number 15 on the Country Songs chart. Amazingly, "Fearless" was the first song in Billboard history to be certified gold before it was officially released.

2. "FIFTEEN"

BEHIND THE MUSIC Taylor started writing this song with the lines, "Abigail gave everything she had / to a boy who changed his mind," which even critics who weren't head over heels for the album singled out as "a great, revealing line about a friend's lost innocence."

BETWEEN THE LINES Taylor is often praised for speaking authentically about people her age. Fellow country star Vince Gill said, "Every kid relates to Taylor and those songs because they're pointed right at them," and "Fifteen" is a great example of that. It looks back on those vulnerable years at the beginning of high school when you feel like an outsider and social status can feel like it's everything, when love is the best thing and the worst thing that can happen, when you have no idea where you're headed or who you'll become.

Miley and Taylor at the 51st Annual Grammy Awards on February 8, 2009, after performing "Fifteen."

"Fifteen" offers great advice for those tumultuous times: this too shall pass. Taylor wisely advised, "Don't make high school everything. Because if high school is everything, then you've got a long life to live, and I'd like to think that the best years of my life are still ahead of me." Taylor further explained, "It says, 'I should have known this, I didn't know that, here's what I learned, here's what I still don't know.'" Taylor skillfully weaves together the two themes of the song — fitting in and falling in love — in one line, "When all you wanted was to be wanted," getting to the heart of a teenager's longing to belong.

AUDIENCE OF ONE "I think that the song 'Fifteen' is definitely advice to my former self, but it could also be advice to any girl going into ninth grade and feeling like you're the smallest person on the planet," said Taylor.

FUN FACTS In the summer of 2008, the guy who hurt Abigail came back into her life with a grand gesture: he asked her to come talk to him, and he was waiting in a field, inside a heart made of candles with a big bouquet of roses for her. Taylor even lent a hand to the one-time heartbreaker, telling him all of Abigail's favorite songs so he could put them on a mix CD. But even when life seems as perfectly orchestrated as a romantic movie, love isn't easy, and Taylor admitted, "As usual, I had to clean up the mess the next day . . . But that's okay. I didn't mind."

DIARY DECODER "I cried while recording this" lets listeners know that this is a song that made Taylor shed some teardrops on her guitar.

CHARTING SUCCESS "Fifteen" peaked at number seven on the Hot Country Songs chart, number 10 on the Pop Songs chart, number 23 on the Hot 100, and also appeared on the Hot Adult Contemporary and the Hot Adult Pop Songs list. Though the song may contain advice for freshmen, adults relate to it too!

3. "LOVE STORY"

BEHIND THE MUSIC Taylor wrote this song lying on her bedroom floor in a mere 20 minutes and recorded a rough cut of the track in 15 minutes of studio time the next day. She said the song sprang from the line "This love is difficult / but it's real," and she noted on her MySpace, "When I wrote that line, I knew it would be my favorite line to sing every night. And it's true, every time I sing that, I can't help but smile."

BETWEEN THE LINES "Love Story" follows the plot of *Romeo and Juliet* fairly faithfully. Taylor's Juliet is on a balcony remembering when she met Romeo, which in Shakespeare's play is also at a party. The two lovers meet again in a garden (in the play it's an orchard), and Romeo must leave town, though in the song it's because Juliet's family disapproves, whereas in *R&J* there's a more serious reason — Romeo kills Juliet's cousin, Tybalt. Taylor's love story ends with a happy ending in marriage, and though Romeo and Juliet marry in Shakespeare's tale, it is done hastily and in secret without either family's approval.

Discussing her rewrite of the famous double-suicide finale, Taylor said, "I was really inspired by that story. Except for the ending. I feel like they had such promise and they were so crazy for each other. And if that had just gone a little bit differently, it could have been the best love story ever told. And it is one of the best love stories ever told, but it's a tragedy. I thought, why can't you . . . make it a happy ending and put a key change in the song and turn it into a marriage proposal."

There's a second literary reference in "Love Story" in the line "'Cause you were Romeo, I was a scarlet letter." *The Scarlet Letter* is a famous novel by Nathaniel Hawthorne about Hester Prynne, a woman who cheated on her husband and is outcast from her community. Though Taylor's Juliet has been faithful, the connection is that, like Hester, Juliet is in an unpopular relationship that upsets the people around her. In the end, the message of this uplifting love anthem comes down to Taylor's favorite line, which means to her that "sometimes you have to fight for love, but sometimes it's worth fighting for."

AUDIENCE OF ONE Taylor told *Time* that this one's about a guy she never really dated (she calls these boys "nominees") because her friends and family didn't approve. But no doubt her would-be Romeo approves of the happy ending Taylor made up for them.

FUN FACTS "Love Story" has already been covered by many artists including Intohimo, The Scene Aesthetic, Forever the Sickest Kids, Davedays, Tiffany Giardina, and Savannah Outen and Josh Golden. Fittingly, "Love Story" plays in the trailer for the 2010 film *Letters to Juliet*.

DIARY DECODER The secret message here is "Some day I'll find this." Even though Taylor's happy when she's single and despite having had her share of heartbreak, she still believes in love. She told *Seventeen*, "I have to believe in fairytales, and I have to believe in love — but not blindly. If you do meet your Prince Charming, know he is going to have his good days and his bad days. He is going to have days when his hair looks horrible, and days when he's moody and says something that hurts your feelings. You have to base your fairytale not upon happily ever after, but on happy right now."

CHARTING SUCCESS Listeners across the globe officially fell in love with "Love Story." The song charted in Australia, Austria, Belgium, Canada, Denmark, France, Germany, Greece, Ireland, Japan, Mexico, the Netherlands, New Zealand, Norway, the Philippines, Spain, Sweden, Switzerland, and the United Kingdom. In the U.S., the single topped the Hot Country Songs, Top 40 Mainstream, and Hot Adult Contemporary Tracks charts, as well as hit number three on the Adult Pop Songs chart and number four on the Hot 100. With over four million downloads, "Love Story" was the most downloaded country song in history, and tied Lady Gaga's "Just Dance" for the highest number of downloads for a song by a female artist. In 2008, it won Billboard's Hot Radio Songs of the Year award, and in 2009, it won Country Song of the Year at the BMI Awards, Music Video of the Year at the CMA Awards, and Video of the Year and Female Video of the Year at the CMT Music Awards.

4. "HEY STEPHEN"

BEHIND THE MUSIC Taylor penned this playful love song for her crush, Stephen Barker Liles, guitar player and vocalist for Love and Theft. The band opened for Taylor as part of her '08 tour, so it's likely this one was written on the road.

BETWEEN THE LINES This song is like a secret love letter, right from the opening greeting of "Hey Stephen." Some of Taylor's cherished romantic images return, including kissing in the rain and showing up at someone's bedroom window. If all these songs were based on real moments, Taylor's bedroom window would get as much traffic as Dawson Leery's; this romantic gesture also appears in "Our Song," "Love Story," and "Come In with the Rain." And though Taylor insists she never wants to write songs only about being on the road, there's just a hint of it here. The line "Hey Stephen, why are people always leaving? / I think you and I should stay the same" suggests that a life on the road sometimes means too many goodbyes.

AUDIENCE OF ONE When *Fearless* came out, Taylor texted Stephen saying, "Hey, track 5!" and was rewarded with an email reply from her overwhelmed crush. Stephen told *People*, "We've become great friends since Love and Theft started opening shows for her. I think everyone would agree she's a total sweetheart and anyone would be lucky to go out with her." For a snippet of Taylor with Stephen, watch her October 19, 2008, MySpace video to see them lip-synch to Katy Perry's "Hot N Cold."

FUN FACTS The finger snaps on this track are provided by Martina McBride's children and their friends, who were dying to meet Taylor, and jumped at the opportunity during a recording session at John McBride's Blackbird Studio.

DIARY DECODER "Love and Theft" reveals who the mystery Stephen is. The band released their debut album, *World Wide Open*, in 2009 and a self-titled follow-up in 2012.

5. "WHITE HORSE"

BEHIND THE MUSIC According to *Country Weekly*, this song was written with the guy from "Love Story" in mind. After Taylor composed the first verse, she called Liz Rose, and in about 45 minutes the pair polished off the song that would go on to win a Grammy.

BETWEEN THE LINES For pessimists, "White Horse" could be "Love Story: Part 2." It's a song about the end of a relationship with no hope for recovery. Taylor explained to *Billboard*, "It's one of the songs that I am really proud of on the record because it's so sparse — guitar, piano, and cello . . . it talks about falling in love and the fairytales that you are going to have with this person, and then there is that moment where you realize that it is not going to happen. That moment is the most earth-shattering moment." Of course, "I'm not a princess / This ain't a fairytale" doesn't mean that true love doesn't exist, just not between

these two. Interestingly, Taylor mentions the "face of an angel" in this song, which is also part of the chorus in "Hey Stephen." Hopefully Stephen wasn't the one to let her down!

FUN FACTS Originally "White Horse" was going to be saved for Taylor's third album because *Fearless* already had its fair share of sad songs. That decision changed when *Grey's Anatomy* wanted the song for the premiere episode of season five, "Dream a Little Dream of Me." And while "White Horse" may be about disappointment, for Taylor having a song on her favorite show was a dream come true: "You should've seen the tears streaming down my face when I got the phone call that they were going to use that song. I have never been that excited. This is my life's goal, to have a song on *Grey's Anatomy*. My love of *Grey's Anatomy* has never wavered. It's my longest relationship to date."

DIARY DECODER "All I ever wanted was the truth" hints that Taylor's prince was a liar and that their fairytale castle wasn't built on solid ground.

CHARTING SUCCESS This song earned Taylor two Grammy Awards — one for Best Country Song and one for Best Female Country Vocal Performance. This second single from *Fearless* peaked at number two on the Billboard Hot Country Songs chart, number 13 on the Hot 100, and number 23 on the Pop 100, and also charted in Canada, the United Kingdom, and Australia. The "White Horse" single received platinum certification.

6. "YOU BELONG WITH ME"

BEHIND THE MUSIC Taylor's inspiration for this song came from eavesdropping while hanging out on her band's bus. Taylor told *Self*, "The guy was going, 'Baby, of course I love you more than music, I'm so sorry. I had to go to sound check. I'm so sorry I didn't stay on the phone.' So immediately in my head, I get this line, 'You're on the phone with your girlfriend she's upset. She's going off about something that you said.' And it all came to me at once. I bolted to my bus [to write it down]." Taylor took the idea to a songwriting session with Liz where the two fleshed out the story, and Taylor notes that "She wears short skirts, I wear T-shirts" was their favorite line to write.

BETWEEN THE LINES Taylor says she never had a crush on her band member; she just inserted herself into the situation and ran with it. But she does know what it's like to be the invisible girl, as she explored in "Teardrops on My Guitar." She explained, "Basically like 'girl-next-door-itis.' You like this guy who you have for your whole life, and you know him better than she does but somehow the popular girl gets the guy every time."

DIARY DECODER "Love is blind so you couldn't see me" is a clever reinforcement of the idea that it's often hard to see the good thing right in front of you.

CHARTING SUCCESS The third single from *Fearless*, "You Belong with Me," was nominated for Song of the Year, Record of the Year, and Best Female Pop Vocal Performance at the 2010 Grammys, although it didn't win. It had better success at the 2009 MTV Video Music Awards where it won Best Female Video. "You Belong with Me" became Taylor's fourth number one hit in the U.S., topping the Hot Country Songs chart and the Hot Adult Contemporary Tracks chart, and scored a number three on the Canadian Hot 100. It also sat at number two on the Pop Songs chart and on the Hot 100, and charted in top 100s all over the world, including in Ireland, New Zealand, and the U.K. "You Belong with Me" has been certified double platinum.

7. "BREATHE"

BEHIND THE MUSIC Taylor admired Colbie Caillat's first album, *Coco*, so much she was determined to work with her fellow up-and-coming artist. She approached Colbie's management, and Colbie ended up with a day off after a radio-station promotional show in Nashville. After working on some pieces Taylor had written, the two wrote "Breathe" together and Colbie contributed vocals, recorded at Starstruck Studios. Taylor gushed to MTV, "I just think she's the coolest thing out there right now. So for her to be on my next album makes me feel cooler." Colbie has nothing but praise for Taylor: "She is so sweet, so beautiful, so talented, and honestly just a really intelligent young women. She knows what she is doing and she knows how to handle her career and take charge. I love her."

BETWEEN THE LINES Before "Breathe," all of Taylor's songs about breakups fell into two categories: laced with anger (like "Picture to Burn" and "Should've Said No") or sad laments about being let down (as in "White Horse" and "Forever & Always"). This downtempo duet explores an ending with no rage and no one to blame; it's about the end of a friendship. She explains, "It's a song about having to say goodbye to somebody, but it never blames anybody. Sometimes that's the most difficult part. When it's nobody's fault."

FUN FACTS "Breathe" shares a title with a

famous song by one of Taylor's favorite performers — Faith Hill. Faith's 1999 single was a huge country and pop hit, landing number ones on three different charts. While Colbie didn't win a Grammy for this collaboration with Taylor, she had one in her pocket thanks to her 2009 duet with Jason Mraz on "Lucky." DIARY DECODER "I'm sorry I'm sorry I'm sorry" is both the secret message and the soft closing vocals that Taylor added while recording, saying to Colbie, "You never said it in the song, but that's totally what the song's about." The apology is not about taking the blame but rather a wish that things turned out differently. CHARTING SUCCESS "Breathe" was nominated for Best Pop Collaboration with Vocals at the 2010 Grammy Awards.

8. "TELL ME WHY"

BEHIND THE MUSIC Sick of getting mixed signals from a guy, Taylor arrived at a writing session with Liz all riled up and vented to her co-writer. Liz asked, "If you could say everything you were thinking to him right now, what would you start with?" Taylor told her, "I would say to him, 'I'm sick and tired of your attitude, I feel like I don't even know you.'" She remembered, "I just started rambling, and she was writing down everything that I was saying, and so we turned it into a song." BETWEEN THE LINES "Tell Me Why" is about a romance gone wrong where the person isn't who she wants him to be and is the kind of guy who makes others feel small to feel better about himself, only acting sweet to stop his girlfriend from leaving. Despite all the song's hurt and disappointment, it ends on a positive note as she walks away from a poisonous relationship.

FUN FACTS "Tell Me Why" shares its title with a 1964 Beatles song that has a similar theme of someone stuck in a miserable relationship: "Did you have to treat me oh so bad / All I do is hang my head and moan." DIARY DECODER "Guess I was fooled by your smile" reminds Taylor's fans that appearances can be misleading.

9. "YOU'RE NOT SORRY"

BETWEEN THE LINES Much like "White Horse," "You're Not Sorry" is about a would-be Prince Charming who's fallen from his pedestal. "It is about this guy who turned out to not be who I thought I was. He came across as Prince Charming. Well, it turned out Prince Charming had a lot of secrets that he didn't tell me about. And one by one, I would figure them out. I would find out who he really was." The discoveries were unpleasant, and Taylor noted, he "kept apologizing and kept doing the same thing over and over again. And after a while I think you just have to stand up to that person and say, 'You're not sorry, at all.'" As the saying goes, "Fool me once, shame on you. Fool me twice, shame on me." FUN FACTS Taylor *and* her music appeared on *CSI* in the episode "Turn, Turn, Turn," which features a remixed version of "You're Not Sorry." DIARY DECODER "She can have you" hints that her boyfriend's greatest secret was another woman. CHARTING SUCCESS Released as a digital single, "You're Not Sorry" climbed to number 11 on the Billboard Hot 100 within a week of its release. Proof that Taylor can spin her heartache into gold: the RIAA gave this song its gold record in 2009.

Colbie Caillat and Taylor at the BMI's 57th Annual Pop Awards on May 19, 2009.

10. "THE WAY I LOVED YOU"

BEHIND THE MUSIC Taylor came up with the concept of a song about dating the good guy while still crushing on the bad guy, and then approached legendary songwriter and musician John Rich with it. "He was able to relate to it because he is that complicated, frustrating messy guy in his relationships. We came at the song from different angles. It was just so cool to get in a room and write with him because he really is an incredible writer," explained Taylor.

BETWEEN THE LINES "The Way I Loved You" explores the strange logic of love where what's bad for you can seem so good. "It's about being in a relationship with a nice, punctual, practical, logical guy and missing the crazy, complicated, frustrating guy," said Taylor. Notice the different texture of instrumentation — string instruments and softly plucked banjo for the good guy versus electric guitar and a more rock 'n' roll drumbeat for the bad boy. By the end, the bad boy's sound takes control of the song and maybe Taylor's heart. Taylor takes some of the blame for things going wrong, singing "I'm so in love that I acted insane." The bittersweet message is "breaking down and coming undone" is just part of the wild ride of love.

FUN FACTS Co-writer John Rich, a Nashville musician, songwriter, and producer, played with the band Lonestar for eight years before embarking on a solo career, then becoming one half of the country duo Big & Rich. John's a prolific songwriter and has published over 100 songs, writing for artists such as Martina McBride, Faith Hill, and Bon Jovi.

On working with a co-writer 15 years his junior, he said, "Sure there's an age difference, but she knows herself and her audience very well, and she's so connected to who that audience is. She knows she's still a kid and embraces it. She writes things that are important to her. If she breaks up with a boyfriend, that's traumatic to her, and she'll write about it. Just like if I'm pissed off at the news, I'll write 'Shuttin' Detroit Down.' But we respect that about each other."

DIARY DECODER "We can't go back" suggests that while she can't forget "screaming and fighting and kissing in the rain," those roller-coaster highs and lows are a thing of the past.

11. "FOREVER & ALWAYS"

BEHIND THE MUSIC Taylor wrote this song at the *very* end of the recording process, and she had to plead with Scott Borchetta to include it on her album the day before the final version of *Fearless* was submitted.

BETWEEN THE LINES Taylor writes about the confusion and hurt that comes when someone who seemed committed suddenly gets cold and distant. The songwriter explained, "I'd never had that happen to me before that way, with that abruptness. I thought to myself, 'This needs to be said.' It's a song about watching somebody completely fade away in a relationship and wondering what you did wrong and wondering why things have changed." Taylor's feelings are evident in the changing tempo of the song; she told the *LA Times*, "That emotion of rejection, for me, usually starts out sad and then gets mad. This song starts with this pretty melody that's easy to sing along with, then in the end . . . I'm basically screaming it because I'm so mad. I'm really proud of that." As in most Taylor Swift songs, rain has a role to play,

this time its more miserable side represents the heartache of being left in the lurch.

AUDIENCE OF ONE This one's for Joe Jonas, with whom she had a very secret relationship and a very public break-up. Asked about the song, Joe Jonas told *Seventeen*, "It's flattering. It's always nice to hear their side of the story." He was less kind in his musical response; the opening verse to the Jonas Brothers' song "Much Better," goes "I get a rep for breakin' hearts / Now I'm done with superstars / And all the tears on her guitar." Ouch.

FUN FACTS The platinum edition of *Fearless* also includes a plaintive piano and cello version of "Forever & Always."

DIARY DECODER "If you play these games we're both going to lose" is the secret message for Joe. With the release of *Fearless: Platinum Edition*, Taylor still didn't have Joe out of her system — the piano version has a different message: "I still miss who I thought he was."

12. "THE BEST DAY"

BEHIND THE MUSIC Taylor wrote this song on the road in the summer and recorded it secretly so she could surprise her mom with it for Christmas.

BETWEEN THE LINES Though Taylor writes a lot of love songs for the guys in her life, this one is for her family, who not only support her in her career but gave her a wonderful childhood. Taylor mined her childhood memories for the first verse, using a child-like voice to capture the essence of those years. The despair of the second verse contrasts with the happiness of the first, but Taylor's mom pulls her through. Her father also gets some love in the song and there's a shout-out to brother Austin, who may

not be famous, but Taylor insists "inside and out he's better than I am." While many of Taylor's songs are filled with anger, loneliness, and pain, "The Best Day" shows us where she got her normally sunshiny attitude.

AUDIENCE OF ONE As if the song wasn't special enough, Taylor put her video editing skills to work and pieced together home videos to the track for her mother as a Christmas present. All the work was worth it for her mom's reaction. Andrea told *Dateline*, "The first time that she played 'The Best Day' for me was Christmas Eve. She had made this edited music video. I'm looking on the TV and this video comes up with this voice that sounds exactly like Taylor's. And I looked over at her and she said, 'I wrote it for you, Mom.' And that's when I lost it. And I've lost it pretty much every time I've heard that song since."

FUN FACTS In May 2009, the video that Taylor created for her mom was made available to fans as part of a special Mother's Day promotion. Fans could go to a Big Machine website and watch the video and send one of three custom e-cards to their mothers.

DIARY DECODER If Taylor's love for her mom wasn't clear enough in the song, the secret message drives it home with "God bless Andrea Swift."

13. "CHANGE"

BEHIND THE MUSIC This song started from Taylor's frustration that being on an independent label meant she'd have to work twice as hard to get media attention, get on a tour, and get nominated for awards. "There were times I was working so hard that I didn't realize that every single day our numbers were getting big-

FEARLESS: PLATINUM EDITION

Less than one year after *Fearless* was released, the millions of fans all over the world who had bought that album wanted more. Following the precedent of her first album, Taylor released the platinum edition of *Fearless* on October 26, 2009. It had six new tracks as well as Taylor's videos, behind-the-scenes featurettes on the making of her videos and the Fearless Tour, her CMT Awards "Thug Story" video, and concert photos taken by her brother, Austin. The album's first new track, "Jump Then Fall," is a sweet summer love story, which Taylor calls "really bouncy and happy and lovey." She debuted the song on *Dancing with the Stars* on October 27, 2009, and it was number one on iTunes the week it was released and climbed to number 10 on the Billboard Hot 100. The next track, "Untouchable," is a dreamy number about having a serious crush on someone you can never be with. And though this song sounds like a Taylor Swift original, it's actually written by Nathan and Cary Barlowe of the rock band Luna Halo. Scott Borchetta suggested the song to Taylor when she needed a cover for her appearance on *Stripped*, and she and songwriter Tommy Lee James adapted it. The performance was so popular on YouTube that Big Machine included it on the *Platinum Edition*. In case Joe Jonas didn't get the message the first time, "Forever & Always" was back in a piano version that shows that when the anger's over, sometimes sadness remains. In "Come In with the Rain," Taylor hopes, even if she shouldn't, that a lost love will return, and "SuperStar" is a musical daydream about a famous guy, causing fans to debate whether Joe Jonas had inspired another track in Taylor's song catalog. The last addition to the platinum edition was "The Other Side of the Door," which picks up after a bad fight and vents the frustration of a person too proud to admit she's wrong. Taylor says the song is "all about the dramatics of a relationship." The new songs continued the theme of being fearless, exploring love, and, most importantly, demonstrated Taylor's love for her fans that will last forever and always.

ger," Taylor recalled. "Every single day, our fan base was growing. Every single day, the work that we were doing was paying off." But since she couldn't see it yet, Taylor set the song aside until she had a sign that things had changed. That happened on the night she won the Horizon Award. Taylor remembered, "When they called out my name as the Horizon Award winner, I looked over and saw the president of my record label crying. Walking up those stairs, it just occurred to me that that was the night things changed. It changed everything." She completed the song the next night, writing lines that acknowledged her new perspective: "It was the night things changed, / do you see it now?"

Taylor with her mother, Andrea, and brother, Austin.

BETWEEN THE LINES The final song on *Fearless* is about challenging expectations and making the impossible possible. For Taylor, it was proving to those non-believing record execs, her teasing classmates, and the industry as a whole that she could not only make it, but rise to the top. Scott Borchetta watched that change happen and noted that this song marks a similar change in her music: "It's one of the few non-love songs that she's recorded so far. Live, it's becoming this tour de force. It's almost like a U2 moment now. So the maturation process is amazing, because she's found a different place where the songs are getting even more important. But it's still her."

AUDIENCE OF ONE This song is for underdogs everywhere. "When I play it, I think about anybody who is on the bottom and knows that someday they want to be somewhere else," said Taylor.

FUN FACTS "Change" was featured on the AT&T Team USA Soundtrack and played during the highlights montage that closed TV coverage of the 2008 Olympic Games.

DIARY DECODER While "The Best Day" offers a thank-you to the Swift family, this hidden message is for Scott Borchetta: "You made things change for me."

CHARTING SUCCESS In the true spirit of the song, "Change" overcame some tough competition on the charts, climbing to number 10 on the Hot 100 list.

CHAPTER 8

THE FEARLESS TOUR

With two platinum albums, singles burning up the charts, and numerous award nominations, there was only one thing missing from Taylor's swift rise to superstardom — a headlining tour. It's not that she hadn't already thought about it; she'd been dreaming about it since she was just a kid. But the clear-headed businesswoman in her realized it was best to wait until she could realize all her big ideas before embarking on the tour. "I never wanted to go into an arena and have to downsize it so there were only 5,000 or 4,000 people there," said Taylor. "So we waited a long time to make sure the headlining tour was everything I wanted the headlining tour to be."

Downsizing wouldn't be necessary. On January 30, 2009, Taylor announced a 52-city headlining tour. The Fearless Tour would start in Evansville, Indiana, and make its way all over America. "Headlining my own tour is a dream come true. This way I can play more music every night than I ever have before," said Taylor in her press release. "Having written my own songs, they are all stories in my head, and my goal for this tour is to bring those stories to life."

The tour was a dream come true for fans as well who rushed out to buy tickets, which sold out within minutes of going on sale. The nearly 40,000 tickets for her show at Madison Square Garden were snapped up within a minute, and the 20,000 for the Staples Center in L.A. within two. It was a surreal experience for Taylor, who, like any artist doing her first headlining tour, was worried about filling seats. She remembered, "The moment I knew I was having a good year was when I got a phone call from the promoter of my tour. He

said, 'I'm about to put your tickets on sale for the first date of your tour.' And I was like, 'Okay, well, let me know tonight how we're doing.' I got a call from him three minutes later saying, 'You sold it out.'"

This unimaginable success was a complete shock to the rising star who confessed, "What I never expected was going out on my first headlining tour and never having to worry about ticket sales. I look at things from a practical place and a very realistic place. I've always had crazy dreams, but I've never expected them to come true."

TAYLOR MADE

Like many musicians, Taylor had been dreaming of her ideal tour for years. She'd been inspired by the artists she'd toured with — Rascal Flatts, Brad Paisley, Tim McGraw and Faith Hill, George Strait, and Kenny Chesney — and noted, "I've been on tour with every single one of my heroes, and I've seen what they do live. Some things have blown me away, and I've taken away some things that I really want to incorporate." Taylor combined what she'd learned from her idols with the plans she'd long had in the making. Many hours had been spent deciding exactly how she wanted things to look and how they would run. She told *Dateline*, "This is absolutely my baby, it's my obsession, it's the thing that I've wanted to do since I was really little, and I've been opening up for people since I was 16, so that's been a long time for me to sit there in my tour bus at night and think what would I do if I actually got to do this?"

Taylor's plans were marked by a theatrical

flair likely left over from her community theater days. She told *Rolling Stone*, "I feel like there's drama that I've always been attracted to — sort of a theatrical type, dramatic performance that I feel is sometimes missing when you see shows these days. I never want people to think that they're just seeing a show where I'm playing song after song after song. When I play a song, I want people to feel like they're experiencing exactly what I went through when I wrote the song as I'm singing it for them."

What kind of theatrics did Taylor dream up? First of all, she wanted to be able to project images onto the entire stage so that what people saw would be changing all the time. It

was an uncommon feature for a country music tour, but to Taylor it was important that "you're never really seeing the same thing visually." The stage also featured a giant screen to play videos like her star-studded "Fearless Is" video and smoke machines to add the necessary moodiness to numbers like "You're Not Sorry." She also ensured that the set was rigged with an elevator to make a dramatic entrance. Some of the numbers also had elaborate sets and costumes. For the opening song, "You Belong with Me," Taylor and her band and dancers dressed up in band uniforms, and midway through, Taylor's was ripped off to reveal a

trademark sparkly dress. During "Love Story," the singer and her dancers donned period costumes, and the entire stage was made to look like a castle. She tossed red chairs in "Forever & Always," and in "Should've Said No" she and Caitlin had a furious drum battle before the song ended with the onstage rain shower that got so much attention at the 2008 ACM Awards. Taylor was also sure to have multiple stage areas so that she could perform all over the arena, even out among the audience. She had up to eight costume changes, some of which took place in front of the crowd! She confessed, "I live for an onstage costume change." Her most dramatic one? A Cinderella-like transition from Renaissance ball gown to wedding dress during "Love Story." Bass player Amos Heller summed the whole production up well: "Anything Taylor wants to happen, happens onstage."

As with everything in her career, Taylor supervised all of the tour preparations from set design to selecting her six dancers. Andrea Swift explained, "Every single decision that's made, whether it's talking about artwork that's going to go on the side of the buses for the tour or a script that needs to be read, you know, almost invariably, someone in the room says, 'Have you checked with Taylor?'" It's a point Taylor isn't ashamed to admit: "I absolutely want to have my hands on everything that has to do with my career."

Yet even though she has total control, Taylor makes sure that she doesn't act like a self-righteous dictator. "There are times when you get frustrated, but the one thing you always focus on is treating people well. You just cannot storm off and freak out. People don't take you seriously if you scream, if you raise your voice, especially when you're a 19-year-old girl," she told *Dateline*.

When all the sets were built, the costumes selected, and the dancers cast, there was still a ton of rehearsing to do before this Taylor-made production was ready to hit the road. Taylor's team rented a warehouse in Nashville where the entire set was erected for three weeks of rehearsals prior to the opening show. "We've got my whole stage set up and have been rehearsing all day, every day. It's like camp. But better," Taylor blogged. "I'm in heaven right now. Constantly having meetings

THE FEARLESS SET LIST

For those who couldn't get tickets in time, here's the set list from the October 1, 2009, show in Pittsburgh, PA, at the Mellon Arena:

1. "You Belong with Me"
2. "Our Song"
3. "Tell Me Why"
4. "Teardrops on My Guitar"
5. "Fearless"
6. "Forever & Always"
7. "Hey Stephen"
8. "Fifteen"
9. "Tim McGraw"
10. "White Horse"
11. "Love Story"
12. "The Way I Loved You"
13. "You're Not Sorry"
14. "What Goes Around"
    (cover of Justin Timberlake's song)
15. "Picture to Burn"
16. "I'm Only Me When I'm with You"
    (with Kellie Pickler and Gloriana)
17. "Should've Said No"

with the video crew and the lighting guys and the carpenters and the band and running through things over and over and over again." After rehearsals in Nashville, the crew moved to Evansville, Indiana, the site of the first show, for a few days of rehearsals there.

Not all of the preparations were for the stage; Taylor made sure that the backstage area would be memorable as well. The "T Party"

MEET THE AGENCY

After Taylor's band filmed the video for "Picture to Burn," they adopted the nickname "The Agency." Meet the agents in Taylor's family away from home.

Al Wilson (bandleader and drums): With a rock, R&B, and Latin jazz background, Al brings a broad musical sensibility to the band. He's been playing with Taylor since he met her in 2006: "As soon as I met her, she has an electricity, an innate sense of rock about her that was cool." Of the band's sound, he told *Dateline*, "This particular 'country pop' band is more rock. It's pretty rock." For a guy who used to go to New York Rangers games at the stadium, playing Madison Square Garden on the Fearless Tour was the pinnacle of his career thus far.

Amos Heller (bass): Amos has been playing bass since he was a 10-year-old in Virginia. In 2005, after a decade of working in the Cincinnati music scene, Amos moved to Nashville and joined Taylor's band while they were on the Brad Paisley tour in late 2007. The thing that impresses Amos the most about Taylor is how she's gone above and beyond what fans would be satisfied with for this tour: "It speaks to her ambition as a performer that she doesn't just want to stand there and play the songs and there you go and goodnight, she wants to *show* people what she means by the songs."

Caitlin Evanson (fiddle, guitar, vocals): Seattle-born Caitlin is a solo artist in her own right. Classically trained in violin, she heard Pearl Jam's "Jeremy" and a whole new world of music opened up to her. She's been in a number of bands since her teen years; Caitlin said she's "always been wired to entertain." It's certainly true of her fiercely energetic performances with Taylor whether she's fiddling, providing vocals, or battling it out on the drums. Caitlin wrote, "Our Taylor has included us [the band], recognized and pushed us to the front, right next to her to be a part of every award she has won this year. CMAs, VMAs, AMAs, ACMs, and pretty much any three-letter ceremonies. I feel like we've lived a thousand lifetimes this year alone. She loves us like family."

Grant Mickelson (lead guitar, vocals): Originally from Iowa, Grant moved to Texas to study music then to Nashville where he worked with other country music artists before joining Taylor's band in 2007. He brings a rock 'n' roll background to his playing, and is grateful to Taylor for allowing him and the band that outlet: "She's not afraid to jump to different genres and music." Through the experiences he's had playing with Taylor, Grant's "dreams have already happened. I have to come up with more dreams. I can't believe I get to do this."

An overwhelmed Taylor is joined onstage by her band at the CMA Awards where she won 2009's Entertainer of the Year. (L to R) Liz Huett, Caitlin Evanson, Paul Sidoti, Grant Mickelson, Amos Heller, and Al Wilson.

Liz Huett (backup vocals): Californian Elizabeth Huett first came to mainstream notice as one of the finalists on 2008's *Dance War: Bruno vs. Carrie Ann* but she made an impression on Taylor long before that. Shortly after "Tim McGraw" was released, Liz lined up to introduce herself to Taylor at a meet-and-great and asked the singer for advice on how to break into the music industry. About a year later Liz met the star again while working for an L.A. country radio station. When she finally moved to Nashville, Liz auditioned to be Taylor's backup singer and couldn't be happier that she landed the gig. Liz admires Taylor's integrity and creativity as an artist: "I'll be a fan forever and it's just so fun to be onstage rocking out with her." After the Speak Now Tour, Liz embarked on other adventures.

Mike Meadows (banjo, guitar, mandolin, keyboard): The self-described "songwriter/performer/producer/cellist/guitarist/bassist/singer" joined Taylor's band for the Fearless Tour, and also works and records with Josh Gracin, the Pat McGee Band, MoneyPenny, and Tailgate South. While on the road with the tour, flying from Australia to Japan, he tweeted, "We are all in shock that this is our lives."

Paul Sidoti (guitar, backup vocals): Ohio native Paul started playing guitar at age five and hasn't stopped. Performing in bands in his teens, he began writing and recording music and, after college, moved to Nashville in 2000. Paul joined The Agency just after "Teardrops on My Guitar" was released. A songwriter himself, Paul says of Taylor, "The first and most important thing about her is that she's a great writer. . . . She's walked into a sound check and starting playing a song, and we're like, 'That's amazing. What is that?' and she's like, 'I'm just making it up.'" Encouraging his Twitter followers to watch the "Fearless" video, Paul wrote, "Yes . . . we are having THAT much fun. I love my job."

room became a backstage oasis for the performers while they were getting ready for a show, and a cool place to bring some lucky fans after the show. Like everything else with the tour, Taylor oversaw the details for the Moroccan themed–room from fabric swatches to the candles Taylor had to hide from the fire marshal. Describing it, Taylor noted, "It looks nothing like backstage. It looks like your living room. The walls are covered in magenta/maroon/gold/purple draped fabric, and the floors are carpeted with oriental rugs on top. There are lanterns hanging from the ceiling and candles everywhere." The room was also equipped with a flatscreen-TV entertainment center, giant couches for napping, a foosball table, and a ping pong table. Taylor's also found a way to keep all her loved ones with her on the road: one area in the T Party room was covered with pictures of her family, Abigail Anderson, Selena Gomez, Kellie Pickler, and the band. "It just makes me smile to have little reminders of where you come from," said Taylor.

What better way to feel at home on the road than to bring one of your best friends with you? Another important part of tour planning is selecting an opening act, and for the Fearless Tour the singer's friend Kellie Pickler would be kicking off the show. Having toured together before, opening for Brad Paisley, Taylor knew that her headlining tour would be that much better with Kellie at her side. Taylor related, "[We're] almost like sisters at this point. She and I will sit in the dressing room 'til 2 or 3 a.m. just talking and painting our nails. It's so much fun to just have another person out on tour with you that you know you're so close with and you've known for a really long time to the point where you really just feel like they're family."

Taylor signed up another opening band:

FEARLESS PRANKSTERS

Taylor and her team's endless preparation means the Fearless Tour runs like a well-oiled machine, but she's still willing to shake things up a bit with some unscheduled hijinks. "We welcome pranking. We almost require it," Taylor told the *Star-Tribune*.

During the final show on the first leg of the tour, T-Swizzle brought some hip hop to Gloriana's country act, sending her dancers out for an impromptu dance party while the band performed. Kellie Pickler couldn't escape the pranking either when the dancers appeared in butterfly and cat costumes. But Taylor had more up her sleeve. When Kellie launched into "Red High Heels," Taylor's male crew members hit the stage dressed up as women in wigs, Kellie Pickler T-shirts, and, of course, the signature red heels. Kellie got her revenge by hiding in Taylor's piano wearing a clown mask while the songstress tried to play "You're Not Sorry" and wondered why her piano sounded funny. Seems Kellie wasn't sorry for that prank! Taylor started singing "Best Days of Your Life," before hugging her pal and continuing the show.

It was during Taylor's short stint opening for Keith Urban over the summer of 2009 that she pulled off what may have been the ultimate prank. When Keith started playing his song "Kiss a Girl," Taylor and three of her band members appeared onstage in full costume and makeup as hard rock band KISS. This unscripted moment was made even sweeter for audience members when other conspirators dressed as Hershey kisses tossed the chocolates into the crowd. But Taylor was the one who was surprised when she got a tweet from the KISS member she'd impersonated: "Ace Frehley tweeted me. Oh. My God. RT @ace_frehley @taylorswift13 saw your prank on YouTube, you looked great in my outfit. ROCK N ROLL!"

four-person country music group Gloriana, who started playing together in 2008 and had a top 15 hit on the Hot Country Songs chart by February 2009. Announcing her decision to bring the band on tour, Taylor wrote, "They're AMAZING and I love their new single, 'Wild at Heart.' I heard it and immediately knew I wanted them on this tour." Not more than a year earlier, people had been saying similar things about Taylor, but now she was the one helping a new act find its audience.

HEADFIRST, FEARLESS: OPENING NIGHT

Months of preparation and years of dreaming culminated on April 23, 2009, in Evansville, Indiana. The opening night of the Fearless

Tour had finally arrived. As Team Taylor gathered in the T Party room before the show, they huddled up for one last heart-to-heart before going on stage. Bandleader and drummer Al Wilson told the group, "I want to say that I have never been so proud to be on stage with people as much as I am with you guys. I'm so proud to be a part of this. This is, tonight, officially a huge new chapter, beginning right now. Life as we know it has changed from 10 minutes from now."

Taylor thanked all the people who helped get her to this incredible moment: "I just want to say that I didn't have a senior class and I didn't have a sorority. You guys are my senior class, and you guys are my sorority, and you guys are my brothers and my sisters, and you guys are the people who are helping me become the person I'm going to be."

Clad in their "You Belong with Me" band costumes, the group marched out on stage, only to be greeted by thousands of voices screaming in unison. "When I hear that high-pitched sound of all those people screaming together, it's like I want to get on stage right now," said Taylor. She was in her element. "I love being onstage. It's one of my favorite things in the world," gushed the performer. "And on this tour, I really focused on entertaining people, doing things they wouldn't expect me to do."

The constant screaming was a good sign that the Evansville crowd was entertained. Coming off stage, dripping wet and wrapped in her purple Taylor Swift robe, Taylor gushed, "The energy was just incredible. The people were, like, freaking out, losing their minds." She was soaked through and freezing cold — the rain at the end of "Should've Said No" wasn't heated water — but Taylor felt that stormy moment had been the best in the show: "The highlight for me was the rain . . . I've done that once at an awards show, but never in front of a concert crowd and it was so crazy. It was so much fun getting to do that."

Always the perfectionist, even after her stellar performance Taylor had elements she wanted to improve. "I have a lot of notes for lighting and stuff," she mentioned after she came offstage in Evansville. That perfectionism, applied to every possible aspect of the performance, meant that fans across America would get the fairytale performance Taylor dreamed of. Kellie Pickler sums up her bestie best: "She puts on an incredible show. Every night she puts her heart and soul into every performance. And the fans, they know that about her, so I don't think anyone's left the show disappointed."

LIFE ON THE ROAD

With over 50 scheduled shows in the first leg of the tour alone, Taylor had a jam-packed six months ahead. And though a rock star lifestyle may seem glamorous, Taylor's duties went far beyond putting on an incredible show every night. A regular day includes five or six interviews and a meet-and-greet session starting at 5 p.m. before the show's 8 p.m. start. She also greets winners of radio contests or people pulled from the nosebleed sections. "My brain does get fried, but I never get tired of this," she told *Women's Health*. These long days mean that Taylor's tour schedule usually alternates between four-day runs of shows and a few

days off, so she can rest and be ready to give her all in the next set of performances.

One thing that makes long stretches on the road easier is Taylor's custom-made tour bus. When she was an opening act, she shared a bus with her entire band, but now she has a bus for just her and her mom that she designed herself. It has a sitting area swathed in plum and gold–colored plush fabrics, bunk beds with fold-down flatscreen TVs, and even a working fireplace! On the door, Taylor's lucky 13 is painted and her motto stretches over an arch: "Never Never Never Give Up."

Having a seriously pimped ride makes time on the road more bearable, but Taylor's number-one comfort through long tour stretches was her mom, who's almost always by her side. She's there for a restorative ice cream binge and *Grey's Anatomy* marathon, or to offer her daughter honest feedback. "If she saw something that could have been better, she's not going to hold it in. She's not going to sugarcoat: it's total honesty," says Taylor. "She was my friend on bad days, but she'd also provide me with the accurate amount of constructive criticism." And despite her mom supervising her career, Taylor is careful to make one thing clear, "My parents are the coolest. My mother is so not a momager."

Occasionally, Taylor's father Scott joins his wife and daughter at shows, bringing his own brand of unconditional support and his great sense of humor. "He's a social butterfly, and loves being on tour. He loves it so much, he thinks it's absolutely hilarious to mess with me and try to embarrass me as much as possible," laughed Taylor.

Life on the road may be exhausting, but Taylor, the overachiever at heart, thrives with an overloaded agenda. "I get really restless when I haven't worked for a day and a half," she admits. "I have a recurring dream that people are lined up next to my bed, waiting for autographs and taking pictures of me."

The Fearless Tour came to an end at the huge Gillette Stadium in Massachusetts on June 5, 2010, and Taylor was stunned that she got to headline there. It was the perfect venue to end a tour that had been a dream for her and her bandmates, who she collectively referred to as "the one true love" in her life. For that final tour date, Taylor secretly made up tour "yearbooks" for the performers and crew, and, as on the last day of school, everyone signed each other's books, relived moments while poring over the photos, and said their bittersweet goodbyes . . . Taylor was headed back to the studio.

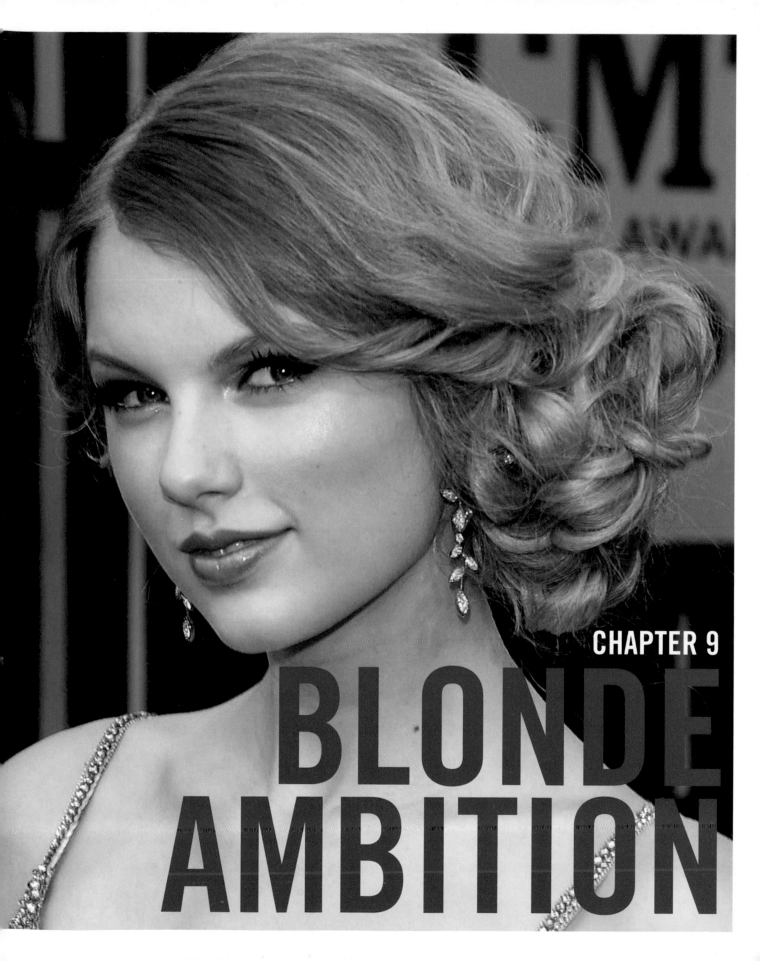

CHAPTER 9

BLONDE AMBITION

In a 2007 interview with *Florida Entertainment Scene*, Taylor was asked where she thought she'd be in five years. The rising star replied, "In five years, I'll be 22. I'd really like to be starting to headline. I think that would be amazing. I'd love to have another platinum album, and I'd love to have won some sort of award (an ACM or CMA, I don't care). Five years is a long time, so who knows what might happen. I never thought all of this would happen in one year, so I can't wait to see my life in five!"

As it turned out, Taylor's career was in fast-forward, and she wouldn't have to wait five years for any of those dreams to come true.

AND THE AWARD GOES TO . . .

Taylor's talents have been recognized at nearly every music award ceremony in America — the ACM Awards, the CMA Awards, the CMT Music Awards, the AMAs, and the Grammys. Her pop success also ensured her a place at the MTV Video Awards, the People's Choice Awards, the Teen Choice Awards, and the Kids' Choice Awards. She's become a regular feature on the red carpet and onstage, where she routinely surprises fans with collaborations (with Def Leppard or T-Pain) and unexpected theatrics (such as the pouring rain shower at the 2008 ACM Awards).

After less than two years on the scene, the young songstress was taking home some of the industry's most prestigious awards. At the 2009 Academy of Country Music Awards, she took home not only Album of the Year for *Fearless* but also the Crystal Milestone Award, which recognizes the most country albums

sold that year. Back in 2007, the Country Music Association had earmarked Taylor as promising new talent in country music by giving her the Horizon Award. Just two years later, the CMA confirmed their prediction. At the ceremony in November 2009, Taylor took home Album of the Year and three other awards, though all of those were eclipsed by the evening's greatest honor — the Entertainer of the Year Award, previously won by artists like George Strait, Garth Brooks, Shania Twain, the Dixie Chicks, Tim McGraw, and Kenny Chesney. Taylor was the youngest person ever to win the prestigious award, and the first female solo artist to do so in almost a decade (since her hero Shania Twain in 1999). Accepting her award, which was presented to her by Faith Hill and Tim McGraw, the overcome performer gushed, "I'll never forget this moment, because at this moment everything that I have ever wanted just happened to me."

After her historic win, Taylor related to *Billboard*, "I'd have to say that was the most mind-blowing experience, hearing my name called and winning that award. That is an award I had placed in an unattainable spot in my head. To be the youngest to win it makes me love country music even more," and she notes, "We wished for this, my parents and I, every single day without actually believing it would come true."

After winning over 50 music industry awards, one still evaded the celebrated songstress: a Grammy. She'd been nominated in 2008 for Best New Artist and lost to Amy Winehouse. When the nominations for the 2010 Grammy Awards were announced, Taylor had eight new chances to earn the cov-

eted golden gramophone. With nominations in both country and mainstream categories, Taylor was competing against hot pop acts like Beyoncé and Lady Gaga. At the end of the night, Nashville's golden girl had proven up to the challenge. Early in the evening, the surprised young star held her first Grammy when she accepted her award for Best Female Country Vocal Performance for "White Horse," and she exclaimed, "This is my first Grammy, you guys! This is a Grammy."

Taylor became pretty familiar with the award before the evening was over. She followed with another award for "White Horse" in the category of Best Country Song; Best Country Album for *Fearless*; and most impressively, the night's most coveted award, Album of the Year. Accepting the award, the ecstatic songstress was sure to thank her parents, and collected herself to emphasize, "All of us, when we're all 80 years old and we are telling the same stories over and over again to our grandkids, and they're so annoyed with us, this is the story we're going to be telling over and over again — in 2010, that we got to win Album of the Year at the Grammys."

Unfortunately, Taylor's Grammy glory was somewhat tainted by a critical backlash to her

singing at the ceremony. Music critics noted that she was off-key during her performances, which included her new single "Today Was a Fairytale" and two collaborations with the legendary Stevie Nicks on "Rhiannon" and "You Belong with Me." Scott Borchetta came to his golden girl's defense, noting that Taylor was having technical problems that prevented her from hearing the complete vocal mix of her duet with Stevie. (Taylor was not the only performer who experienced pitch problems that night.) Scott also stated, "Maybe she's not the best technical singer, but she is the best emotional singer because everybody else who gets up there and is technically perfect, people don't seem to want more of it," adding, "No one is perfect on any given day. Maybe in that moment, we didn't have the best night, but in the same breath, maybe we did."

While *Spin* music critic Alan Light was a part of the negative chorus, he also remarked that a less-than-perfect performance is at least a guarantee of authenticity in an age when most young performers lip-synch. "The fact that it's not perfect, in some ways, has been an asset," he noted. "That makes it all the more believable, to a certain point." That said, he stressed that a performer of Taylor's celebrity needs to work on her television performances, and Scott Borchetta assured the media that Taylor would do just that. "She's a very intelligent girl," said the record executive. "She's going to keep addressing it and keep getting better." Considering Taylor's extraordinary drive and determination, there's no doubt that's true, and that Taylor has many more award wins (and fantastic performances) ahead of her.

INDEPENDENT WOMAN

Taylor may be a fiercely independent musician, but, as a 20-year-old, she was a little behind in striking out on her own. Taylor was happy to remain in Hendersonville living with her parents for the beginning of her career and told *People*, "[My parents] give me space, but I've still got people to talk to when I get lonely." But in September 2009 she revealed that she'd bought her first apartment — a 4,062-square-foot penthouse in Nashville. Since she'd thought about becoming an interior designer when she was younger, having a blank slate of her own was a dream come true. She recalled, "I looked at this place and said, 'The view is amazing. Let's change everything else.'" Her Taylor-made changes include bright colors, handpicked antiques, and some very special custom installations, such as a giant birdcage and a pond filled with koi. Taylor told Oprah, "I love more of an old world, eclectic feel with mismatched chairs and a different knob on every cabinet." When it was completed, Swifty and her friends started calling it "The Imaginarium," Taylor explained, "because it has all of these crazy whimsical things in it." Since that first real estate buy, Taylor has invested in a place in L.A..

Since living alone can be lonely, in November 2011, Taylor found herself a roommate: a Scottish fold kitten named Meredith, after Meredith Grey, the titular doctor from Taylor's favorite *Grey's Anatomy*. Even with Meredith's trademark terrible posture, the adorable cat became universally adored. In July 2012, E!Online even put her at number one on their list of the 100 best things in pop culture, calling her "forged in the great Furnace of Cuteness, infused with the power to wipe out all celebrity pets who dare stand in her path." With Meredith at her side, Taylor has embraced her new solo living. She joked with Chelsea Handler, "Living alone you can do so many fantastic things. You can walk around and have conversations with yourself and, like, sing your thoughts . . . I think I'm the only one who does that."

She has caught up with her college-age friends in terms of living arrangements, but does the singer-songwriter have any plans to enter the hallowed halls of academia herself?

Not for the time being. Taylor told CMT, "Right now, I'm pursuing my career. I always thought that I would go to college, most definitely. But then I really thought about it and assessed the situation, and I can't leave this life. Going to college would mean saying goodbye to my music career, and I just can't do that. There just wouldn't be enough time in the day to be on tour, do interviews, meet-and-greets, TV appearances, and everything else that I need to do and go to college. Maybe later on in life I'll end up taking a few classes or doing it online. But right now, it just isn't where I need to be."

As for her music career, Taylor has multi-platinum albums, international tours that sell out in minutes, and more awards than most artists earn in a lifetime. What other goals could she possibly have left to achieve? "As soon as I accomplish one goal, I replace it with another one," she explained to VH1. "I try not to get too far ahead of myself. I just say to myself, 'All right, well, I'd like to headline a tour,' and then when I get there, we'll see what my next goal is."

It's hard to set new goals when Taylor's entire career has exceeded her wildest dreams. When Oprah asked her if her life was as she'd imagined it would be, Taylor had a simple answer: "It's better."

SPEAKING UP

"The second that I put out *Fearless*, the moment that album came out and I was done with it, I started writing for my next album," said Taylor in December 2009. "I love to plan 20 steps ahead of myself, and it's [a] really fun competition game that I play with myself, trying to top what I've done last. For this next record, that's all that I've been thinking about, that's all that my mind has been fixated on for the last year, and it's all I'm going to be thinking about for this next year."

One way Taylor pushed herself on the record was by writing all the songs completely solo. Though she'd written alone on some tracks in the past (like "Love Story," "Fifteen,"

"Should've Said No," and "Our Song"), she'd worked with co-writers for most of her debut album and six of the tracks on *Fearless*. She called writing alone a "natural progression" and explained, "There was a flow that just kind of happened. I would get inspired to write songs at the most inconvenient times, three in the morning or in the middle of a meet-and-greet or in the middle of a conversation with my friends, and I'd just drift off. And they're like, 'Oh, you're working again, aren't you?'" Writing alone gave Taylor new freedom but new pressure, and she noted, "I take full responsibility for every word and every verse of every song on the record. It's scary, adventurous, and wonderful at the same time."

What may have been more intimidating

than writing alone was the lyrical content of these songs, her most personal work yet. She called the album "a collection of confessions" and the songs "open letters," each written for an audience of one. After a tumultuous two years that saw Taylor find unprecedented success and, with it, unprecedented challenges, the songs explore heartbreakers, critics, thieves of moments and of boyfriends. As always, these songs were Taylor's way of processing the events that affected her deeply. "The songs on the record that are really raw," said Taylor, "those songs helped me more than anything." The album became guided by the idea of speaking up, of saying what needed to be said. In her liner notes, Taylor wrote, "In real life saying the right thing at the right moment is beyond crucial. So crucial, in fact, that most of us start to hesitate for fear of saying the wrong thing at the wrong time. But lately what I've begun to fear more than that is letting the moment pass without saying anything. . . . I think the words you stop yourself from saying are the ones that will haunt you the longest."

When it came time to record, Taylor returned to familiar territory, working with Nathan Chapman. She told *Country Weekly*, "With this album, the majority of the songs were recorded in Nathan's basement. I would write songs, drive to his house, and we would build the track from the ground up and at that point we would establish a vibe from what that song needed. We would pick and choose different musicians to come in and play on those songs based on the vibe we wanted, the sounds we wanted, and what we felt they could bring. A lot of times we got a magical first-take vocal and we would keep it . . . it

was a great selection process for the songs before you take it to the big studio." Nathan, who has been by Taylor's side for every album, noted a real progression in *Speak Now*: "She left home, she's living on her own now, and she's seeing the world in a different way after growing up a bit. There's probably some more grown-up things that she's dealing with, and that comes out in the songs."

Fans got their first taste of the new material with the release of "Mine," which shot to number three on the Hot 100. "Mine" is fairly traditional Swifty fare, but at the 2010 VMAs, Taylor sent her first buzzworthy open letter, "Innocent" for Kanye West, who was also performing that night. Taylor wanted to share even more songs, so she previewed three tracks in the weeks leading up to the album's release: on October 4, "Speak Now" hit iTunes, followed by "Back to December" on October 11, and the plucky banjos and feisty finger shaking of "Mean" on October 18. The Taylor Nation also got to sample 30 seconds of "The Story of Us" on October 22, thanks to an arrangement with Comcast On Demand and XfinityTV.com.

On October 25, 2010, *Speak Now* hit the shelves. In its first week, it sold 1,047,000 copies, the second highest sales for a female artist ever, and it stole the top slot on the Billboard 200 chart. Within six weeks of its release, *Speak Now* was certified triple platinum. For the most part, critics looked on Taylor's third effort favorably. *Entertainment Weekly* noted, "*Speak*'s 14 tracks are perfectly contained snow globes of romance and catharsis, whole cinematic narratives rendered in four- to six-minute miniatures. . . . Beneath Swift's not-a-girl, not-yet-a-woman sweetness lurks a rigorous and very skillful technique; love may confound her, but the art of expert songcraft clearly doesn't." *Rolling Stone* praised, "She's in a class by herself when it comes to turning all that romantic turmoil into great songs. At this point, she's like the new Morrissey, except with even more eyeliner." *The New York Times* was effusive calling *Speak Now* "a bravura work of nontransparent transparency . . . the most savage of her career, and also the most musically diverse. And it's excellent too, possibly her best." Even the more restrained *Guardian* review saw much worth commending: "At times the self-consciousness of an artist forcing herself into new modes shows — but mostly, *Speak Now* is a triumph." *Speak Now* also earned a place on many best-of-the-year lists, landing at (lucky) number 13 for *Rolling Stone*, number 10 for the *Washington Post*, and a remarkable number two for the *New York Times*. And thanks to her courageous solo writing, all this praise and success belonged, clearly and indisputably, to the 20-year-old Taylor Swift.

CHAPTER 10

SPEAK NOW
SWIFT NOTES

1. "MINE"

BEHIND THE MUSIC The inspiration behind this song was a real-life by-the-water embrace. Taylor told Yahoo!Music, "I saw the entire relationship flash before my eyes, almost like some weird science-fiction movie." When Taylor had worked out the song, she went to Scott Borchetta's office and played it for him. Borchetta recalled, "We probably played that song four or five times. I'm jumping around playing air guitar, she's singing the song back to me, and it was just one of those crazy, fun, Taylor teenage moments."

BETWEEN THE LINES "Mine" is a more grown-up version of "Love Story," sharing the same tempo and chorus-verse dynamics of Swifty's biggest hit. Fairytale courtship has evolved into real-world romance, with new signs of intimacy (lying on the couch and a drawer at her boyfriend's house) and problems (2:30 a.m. fights and bills to pay). It's a fuller, more nuanced depiction of a relationship, one that isn't solely heartbreak or first love. Ultimately the message is hopeful: the key to a happy ending is hanging in there when times get tough. Taylor admitted the song is "about my tendency to run from love. It's sort of a recent tendency. I think it's because, for me, every really direct example of love that I've had in front of me has ended in goodbye and ended in breakups and things like that. . . . This song is sort of about finding the exception to that."

AUDIENCE OF ONE Taylor has been coy as usual about this song's subject, but the mystery man knew it was for him. He emailed her the day the song debuted, telling her, "I had no idea . . . I realize I've been naïve."

(NOT SO) FUN FACTS A low-quality illegal bootleg of the song was leaked on August 4, almost two weeks before the scheduled August 16 release of *Speak Now*'s first single. It was an unwelcome surprise for Taylor, who related, "A leak is so out of my comfort zone, but it ended up good in the end. It made me so emotional that I started crying."

DIARY DECODER This coded message spells Toby, likely referring to Toby Hemingway, her costar in the "Mine" music video. Is this a sign that it didn't take much acting to play the video's couple in love?

CHARTING SUCCESS "Mine" entered the charts at number three on the Billboard Hot 100, making Taylor the second artist to have multiple tracks debut in the Top 5 in a single year. (She shares the honor with Mariah Carey.) It also peaked at number two on the Hot Country Songs chart, number one on the Adult Contemporary chart, and at numbers seven and twelve on the Adult Pop Songs and Pop Songs charts respectively. On November 29, 2010, less than three months after its release, "Mine" was certified double platinum. It also took home Video of the Year at the CMT Awards and two song honors at the BMI Awards.

2. "SPARKS FLY"

BEHIND THE MUSIC Though Taylor hasn't been specific about the initial spark for this track, the song is a revamped version of an old one Taylor used to play in concert. Fans kept asking to hear it and insisting it should be on the next record, and the songwriter revisited it.

BETWEEN THE LINES This is a straight-ahead song about attraction, the chorus exploding like fireworks in between the longing of the verses. Along with swapping guitars for banjos, the change from the earlier version is in those verses: the narrator in old version is ready to abandon herself to romance, but in the *Speak Now* rewrite, she's wise enough to know these fireworks might leave her burned.

FUN FACTS "Sparks Fly" was the opening song of the Speak Now Tour: a thank-you to the fans who championed it all along.

DIARY DECODER "Portland, Oregon" is the all-caps message this time, which some people connect to a 2006 concert where Taylor opened for green-eyed Jake Owen in that very city.

CHARTING SUCCESS "Sparks Fly" peaked at number 17 on the Billboard Hot 100 and number one on the Country Songs chart. It was certified gold on November 29, 2011.

3. "BACK TO DECEMBER"

BEHIND THE MUSIC Though Taylor has never hesitated to call out men who have wronged her, in this case, she shows her sense of justice isn't one sided. "Back to December" is her first apology song, one that starts with a conversation that is, according to Taylor, an "almost word-for-word" transcription of one she had in real life.

BETWEEN THE LINES As suggested by the track's title, "Back to December" is a song that finds her returning to the past with regret. The present-day small talk of the opening verse is ghosted by a much more potent image of a last encounter and roses left to die. Those wilted flowers are an anchoring symbol for the song and the relationship. The songwriter explained, "This is about a person who was incredible to me, just perfect to me in a relationship, and I was really careless with him."

AUDIENCE OF ONE There's little doubt this one

Taylor performs "Back to December" in Central Park.

is for Taylor Lautner, whom Swifty dated in 2009. Aside from the December breakup, that "tanned skin" and "sweet smile" is the *Twilight* star to a T. After the 2011 VMA Awards, the

DIARY DECODER The Swift One really wanted to make sure this apology letter found its recipient: this message spells "Tay."
CHARTING SUCCESS "Back to December" reached number six on the Hot 100, number three on the Country Songs chart, and number 11 on the Pop Songs chart. It was certified platinum in the U.S.

4. "SPEAK NOW"

BEHIND THE MUSIC This song came about after hearing a friend's story about her high-school sweetheart engaged to someone else. The songwriter told E!News, "He had met this other girl who was a horrible person. She made him stop talking to his friends, cut off his family ties, and made him so isolated. And, randomly, I was like, 'Oh, are you going to speak now?'" Taylor started fantasizing what she would do in her friend's shoes, and her spontaneous line became the heart of the song, and the album.

BETWEEN THE LINES This song conjures up a dramatic scene that's been the climax of many a movie: the "Speak now or forever hold your peace" line in a wedding ceremony, the line that could end a marriage before it has even begun. Taylor admitted, "I've always been fascinated by that moment in a wedding, because I think it's a metaphor for a lot of times in our life when we're just about to lose something and that's when we realize that we want it, and that's when we realize we have to speak up." While the "Speak up" message sounds like the confessional songstress, the altar-storming scene is an interesting choice for Taylor, who has traditionally written songs that idolize this sacred moment. Yet here she tears down the

still-supportive Lautner headed over to Taylor's show at the Staples Center, where he got to hear his song played for him, with a special dedication for "the boy from Michigan" (Lautner's home state). Looks like the songstress's apology may have been accepted.

FUN FACTS Orchestral accompaniment makes its debut on a Taylor album in this song (and those strings come back for an encore on "Haunted").

traditional trappings of fairytale romance, dismissing the bride in her "gown shaped like a pastry" and noting that the processional sounds "like a death march." Leave it to Taylor to find something even more romantic than a wedding: a runaway groom who escapes with the wedding-crashing rebel he truly adores.

DIARY DECODER "You always regret what you don't say" is a message that applies to the song and to all the true confessions of the album.

5. "DEAR JOHN"

BEHIND THE MUSIC Taylor explained to *People*, "A lot of times when people's relationships end, they write an email to that person and say everything that they wish they would have said. A lot of times they don't push send. This was a tough one to write and I guess putting it on the album was pushing send."

BETWEEN THE LINES Though the title of this mournful ballad could be a direct address, it's also a play on "Dear John" letters. Thought to originate during World War II, these breakup notes from a spouse explain that he or she is moving on. It's a song loaded with regret and disillusionment, not just with the hot-and-cold ladies' man who ensnared her, but with her younger self, another possible subject of that loaded final line, "You should've known."

AUDIENCE OF ONE John Mayer is likely the recipient of this letter. *Rolling Stone* asked him about it, and, in a reversal, he tried to paint Taylor as the bully. He called the track "cheap songwriting," and admitted, "It made me feel terrible. Because I didn't deserve it. I'm pretty good at taking accountability now, and I never did anything to deserve that. It was a really lousy thing for her to do." Hearing that John

Mayer felt "humiliated" by the song, Taylor responded with an eye roll and "Oh, come *on*," on the *Katie* show.

FUN FACTS Taylor is featured on Mayer's 2009 *Battle Studies* album on "Half of My Heart." Her most prominent solo line may have been prescient: "I can't stop loving you." Pal Selena Gomez identified this song and "Last Kiss" as her favorite tracks on the album.

DIARY DECODER "Loved you from the very first day" suggests that our girl believes in love at first sight, even if it disappears just as quickly.

6. "MEAN"

BEHIND THE MUSIC When critics got nasty after Taylor's off-key performance with Stevie Nicks at the 2010 Grammys, Taylor dealt with it like she always does and wrote this rousing rejoinder. It helped her back on her feet, and she told the Associated Press, "It's a song I wrote on a really, really bad day, but it has produced so many happy days for me since."

BETWEEN THE LINES With its prominent banjo and fiddle and verging-on-bluegrass twang, this upbeat number buoys the sadness and vulnerability in its opening lyrics, carrying the song to its empowering finale. It's appropriate for a song about resilience, an "it gets better" song even before its overtly anti-bullying video. Taylor told *People*, "'Mean' is about bullying at a different stage in my life. I'm not at school and I still know what it feels like." In response to some reactions that Taylor shouldn't be thin-skinned about professional criticism, she noted, "There are different kinds of ways to criticize someone. There's constructive criticism, there's professional criticism — and then there's just being mean. And there's

EXCITING! . . . No one's done as much for women's music since JONI MITCHELL!" He changed his tune after her 2010 Grammy performances, posting a scathing review that argued she had killed her career overnight and "consigned herself to the dustbin of teen phenoms." After "Mean" came out, Lefsetz wrote, "If this song is really about me, I wish it were better." Ouch.

FUN FACTS "Mean" got the *Glee* treatment, sung by Mark Salling (Puck) and Dot-Marie Jones (Shannon Beiste) on the third season episode "Props."

DIARY DECODER "I thought you got me" is likely for Lefsetz; Swifty used to tell him, "You get me" all the time.

CHARTING SUCCESS "Mean" peaked at number 11 on the Billboard Hot 100, number two on the Country Songs list, and was certified platinum. It earned her her first CMA Song of the Year award nomination, Choice Country Song at Teen Choice Awards, and, in the ultimate vindication given the song's inspiration, Best Country Song and Best Country Solo Performance Grammys in 2012.

7. "THE STORY OF US"

BEHIND THE MUSIC After a run-in with her ex, Taylor headed home and told her mom, "I felt like I was standing alone in a crowded room." Her words sparked a song, and she headed to her room to develop it further. "The Story of Us" became the last song she wrote for *Speak Now*, and Taylor noted, "After I finished that one, I knew I was done." And how do Taylor and Nathan celebrate wrapping an album? "We just danced around the room and had a dance party," said Taylor. (You can see part of

a line that you cross when you just start to attack everything about a person."

AUDIENCE OF ONE The most likely target for this song is entertainment lawyer and blogger Bob Lefsetz. In 2007, he called the young Swift a better singer than Madonna and by 2009, after attending her show at the Staples Center, enthused, "Last night I saw the future of the music industry, and it was HEARTWARMING and

the adorable dance party on the NBC *Speak Now* Thanksgiving special.)

BETWEEN THE LINES This up-tempo song with a pop-punk influence speeds along, riding on roaring guitars and pert drumbeats, a surprisingly loud song that came out of an awkward silence. Taylor explained, "'The Story of Us' is about running into someone I had been in a relationship with at an awards show, and we were seated a few seats away from each other. I just wanted to say to him, 'Is this killing you? Because it's killing me.' But I didn't. Because I couldn't. Because we both had these silent shields up."

AUDIENCE OF ONE While a little more subtle than "Dear John," according to an interview Taylor did with *USA Today*, this one's a P.S. to that letter, and the guy in question is once again John Mayer.

DIARY DECODER "CMT Awards" points to the June 2010 show that had both Taylor and Mayer performing, and sitting in the same row.

CHARTING SUCCESS The fourth single from *Speak Now* was a modest success, earning a gold certification from the RIAA and hitting number 41 on the Billboard 100 and number 21 on the Pop Songs chart.

8. "NEVER GROW UP"

BEHIND THE MUSIC Feeling a bit lonely on her first night in her brand-new apartment, Taylor penned this letter to her younger self. She told *60 Minutes*' Lesley Stahl, "I walked into this apartment after I bought it and thought, 'Oh man, this is real now. We're all getting older, and soon my parents are going to be older, and then I have to think about grown-up things.'" Crossing that threshold to adulthood meant looking back to what she had left behind.

BETWEEN THE LINES With lyrics that long for the simplicity of younger years, the pared-down instrumentation of "Never Grow Up" suits the return to childhood. Though the song urges kids to never grow up, growing is, of course, inevitable, and Taylor ages in the song itself — from a tiny infant in the opening verse, to a teen embarrassed to be dropped off by her parents, to a young woman moving into her own apartment. It's a wistful song, and, in an album rife with broken hearts and public betrayal, it's a striking ode to innocence.

AUDIENCE OF ONE Though in some ways this is a letter to herself, it's also an encouragement to her younger fans to enjoy where they are right now. Taylor wrote, "Every once in a while I look down and I see a little girl who is seven or eight, and I wish I could tell her all of this. There she is becoming who she is going to be and forming her thoughts and dreams and opinions. I wrote this song for those little girls."

DIARY DECODER "Moved out in July" marks a milestone for Taylor, and the inspiration for this song.

9. "ENCHANTED"

BEHIND THE MUSIC After meeting someone in NYC who made Taylor's heart beat double-time, the songwriter went back to her hotel and penned this song.

BETWEEN THE LINES "Enchanted" spins off from that feeling of connection with someone at an otherwise uncomfortable party and soars into flights of fancy before crashing back down to

SPEAK NOW: THE DELUXE EDITION

When *Speak Now* hit the shelves, Super Swifties didn't have to wait to get their hands on the deluxe edition. Taylor inked a deal with Target that meant the souped-up CD (with Taylor's purple dress turned red on its cover) would be available exclusively at the chain until November 8, when the tracks landed on iTunes. By January 17, 2012, it was available everywhere with six additional songs, the "Mine" video, and a behind-the-scenes featurette.

The new songs kick off with "Ours," a sunny tribute to the buoyant power of love, even in the hardest of times. (In fact, Taylor started writing with "The stakes are high, the water's rough.") "Ours" became the album's sixth and final single and was certified platinum. "If This Was a Movie," co-written with Martin Johnson of Boys Like Girls, is a plea for a lover to come back and work it out, asking for a rain-soaked reunion straight out of a rom-com. The final bonus track, "Superman," isn't about that famous Man in Tights, but someone who appears just as flawless and heroic and has the same tendency to dash off in a minute. The song came out of a comment she made when her crush walked out of a room: "I turned to one of my friends and said, 'It's like watching Superman fly away.'" Acoustic versions of "Back to December" and "Haunted" round out the extra material, and "Mine" got a makeover for pop radio.

reality with the repeated hope that her new crush isn't spoken for. Taylor explained, "Meeting him, it was this overwhelming feeling of 'I really hope that you're not in love with somebody.' And the whole entire way home, I remember the glittery New York City buildings passing by, and then just sitting there thinking, 'Am I ever going to talk to this person again?' And that pining away for a romance that may never even happen, but all you have is this hope that it could, and the fear that it never will."

AUDIENCE OF ONE Adam Young, the one-man electronica act that is Owl City, appears to be the gent who had Taylor wonderstruck — a word she chose deliberately because he'd used it in an email to her. The song hit home, and on Valentine's Day 2011, he released a reply on his website. He wrote, "Everything about you is lovely. You're an immensely charming girl with a beautiful heart and more grace and elegance than I know how to describe. You are a true princess from a dreamy fairytale, and above all, I just want you to know . . . I was enchanted to meet you too." And, as the icing on this Valentine treat, he recorded a cover of "Enchanted," adding his own verse at the end.

FUN FACTS "Enchanted" was originally the title track for *Speak Now*, but according to Scott Borchetta, "We were at lunch, and she had played me a bunch of the new songs. I looked at her and I'm like, 'Taylor, this record isn't about fairytales and high school anymore. That's not where you're at. I don't think the record should be called 'Enchanted.'" This song was also the inspiration for Taylor's fragrance, Wonderstruck, and appeared in a trailer for the 2012 film *The Vow*.

DIARY DECODER In case using "wonderstruck" wasn't enough of a clue, Taylor added another hint: "Adam."

10. "BETTER THAN REVENGE"

BEHIND THE MUSIC After her boyfriend cheated on her, Taylor decided to get her own kind of revenge — not on him, but on the woman he cheated on her with — by writing this insult-ridden takedown. Not Taylor's most graceful moment.

BETWEEN THE LINES Taylor hasn't mustered this much fiery anger since "Picture to Burn," though in this foot-tapping rocker the target isn't a heartbreaking guy, but the girl who stole him. Between the initial scolding intro and the comparison to a pre-school toy-stealer, Taylor likens the other woman to a selfish, grasping child, but goes on to scathingly accuse her of some very adult behavior later in the song.

AUDIENCE OF ONE Actress Camilla Belle, who worked with Joe Jonas on the Jo Bros' "Lovebug" video and later became his girlfriend, is this song's walking target. "Show me how much better you are" is also a response to the Jonas Brothers' 2009 song "Much Better," which made a reference to Taylor then noted "the girl in front of me / She's much better."

DIARY DECODER "You thought I would forget" suggests this particular burn has been smoldering a long time.

11. "INNOCENT"

BEHIND THE MUSIC After the notorious Kanye incident at the VMAs, Taylor took her time processing how she felt and then (naturally) wrote a song about it. "That was a huge, intense thing in my life that resonated for a long time," Taylor told *Billboard*. "It was brought up to me in grocery stores and everywhere I went, and in a lot of times in my life, when I don't know how I feel about something, I say nothing. And that's what I did until I could come to the conclusion that I came to in order to write 'Innocent.' Even then, I didn't talk about it, and I still don't really talk about it. I just thought it was very important for me to sing about it."

BETWEEN THE LINES If "Never Grow Up" is *Speak Now*'s song about leaving childhood behind, "Innocent" picks up that thread, assuring that even if our "firefly catchin' days" are long behind us, we still carry a bit of that innocence with us. The slow ballad has a mournful inflection, but it's hopeful too: everyone has the possibility to "be brand new." The songwriter reflected that writing "Innocent" "taught me a lot about being able to step back from a situation you don't know what to do with, and put yourself in somebody else's shoes." It might have been easier than it seemed to empathize: parts of the song could also apply to Taylor's Grammy performance fallout — when she too knew what it was like to feel the sting of public backlash.

AUDIENCE OF ONE The 32-year-old in question is undoubtedly Mr. West. Some speculate that his 2010 VMA performance of "Runaway" was a self-aware admission of having been quite the opposite of an innocent.

FUN FACTS Taylor performed her song for the first time at the 2010 VMAs, the scene of the crime the year before.

DIARY DECODER A photo of Kanye stealing the mic from her hangs above the fireplace in Taylor's Nashville pad. Its caption is also this song's code: "Life is full of little interruptions." Taylor explained that the photo reminds her that "nothing is going to go exactly the way you plan it to. Just because you make a good plan, doesn't mean that's gonna happen."

12. "HAUNTED"

BEHIND THE MUSIC Taylor woke up in the middle of the night to write about a sudden and terrible realization: that the person she was in love with was drifting away.

BETWEEN THE LINES "It's about being really strung out on a relationship and wishing you had it back, and being tormented by it," explained Taylor to NBC. "Haunted" opens with crashing orchestral swells — an appropriate beginning for the fraught, chaotic emotion in the lyrics about an ex who's gone but far from forgotten. The songwriter noted, "I wanted the music and the orchestration to reflect the intensity of the emotion the song is about, so we recorded strings with Paul Buckmaster at Capitol Studios in Los Angeles. It was an amazing experience — recording this entire big, live string section that I think in the end really captured the intense, chaotic feeling of confusion I was looking for."

FUN FACTS The week the album was released, Taylor and her band went to the spookiest place on the Universal Lot in L.A. — the house from *Psycho* — and performed "Haunted" inside. Taylor's favorite part of the live strings session (her first ever!) for this song and "Enchanted" was when a cello player let her try out his instrument. When Taylor began playing a "very simple progression," the rest of the orchestra joined in. "They were humoring me! I appreciated it."

DIARY DECODER "Still to this day" reveals that this flame hasn't burned out entirely.

13. "LAST KISS"

BEHIND THE MUSIC According to Taylor, this song came out of a "moment of truth" when she admitted that she missed the life, and imagined future, she had with someone.

BETWEEN THE LINES This ballad sways with the weight of longing: for a lost relationship and for that ex who is also pining away. "Going through a breakup, you feel all of these different things," explained Taylor. "You feel anger, and you feel confusion and frustration. Then there is the absolute sadness. The sadness of losing this person, losing all the memories, and the hopes you had for the future."

AUDIENCE OF ONE If "Better Than Revenge" wasn't evidence enough that the Joe breakup still hurt, this song (and its message) makes it clear. July 9, 2008, is the date Taylor flew to Dallas to see a Jonas Brothers concert.

FUN FACTS Internet commentators have noted that the intro to "Last Kiss" is 27 seconds long — the same length as Joe's notorious breakup phone call.

DIARY DECODER This one's a code that Taylor fans will recognize in a heartbeat: "Forever and Always," her song from *Fearless* about Joe.

14. "LONG LIVE"

BEHIND THE MUSIC This song's melody came to Taylor in her dressing room, right before she went out for an encore on the Fearless Tour.

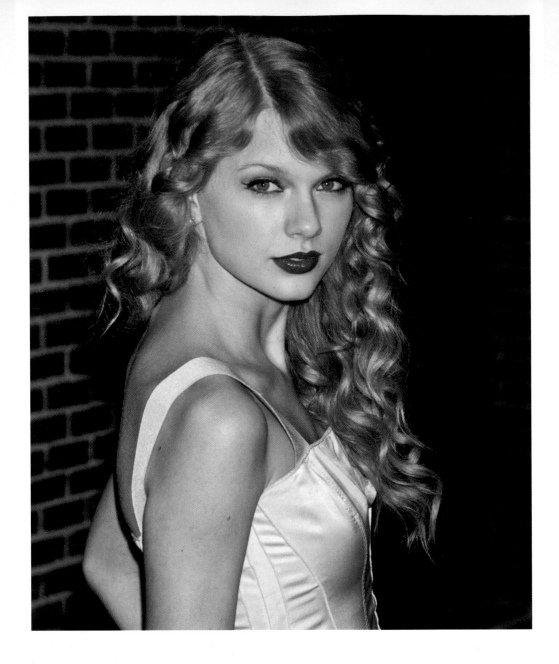

BETWEEN THE LINES Like *Fearless*, *Speak Now* ends with a rousing anthem, and "Long Live" seems to celebrate all the accomplishment "Change" could inspire. The "kings and queens" of this song can savor this moment and their triumph, sure of their legacy. As fans can testify, there's no doubt that Taylor and her crew "will be remembered."

AUDIENCE OF ONE Taylor calls this "sort of the first love song that I've written to my team."

FUN FACTS In 2012, *Rolling Stone* hailed this cut as "the best Bon Jovi song Bon Jovi never wrote."

DIARY DECODER "For you" is a message to all the fans who take the time to look for it and, given the photo underneath the lyrics in her album booklet, to her band.

CHAPTER 11

SPARKS FLY

Just a month after the release of *Speak Now*, Taylor made the big announcement that fans had been hoping for: on November 23, 2010, she let the world know that she "can't wait to get back out and play my new music from *Speak Now* . . . and I'm thrilled to play in new cities around the world and meet even more of my fans." The tour kicked off on February 9, 2011, and over a year and a hundred tour dates later, Taylor and company had played in 17 countries all across Asia, Europe, North America, and Australasia. As with her Fearless World Tour, Taylor worked tirelessly with her team to create a concert experience that her fans wouldn't ever forget — and all that effort made Taylor's tour the top-grossing country music tour of 2011 (at $123.7 million, according to *Billboard*), selling out venue after venue and playing huge stadiums for the first time in her career.

Taylor wanted to bring the stories from the songs on *Speak Now* to life, and she chose an old-world theater look for the stage. Working with the designers and carpenters and costume department, she made sure the "little details . . . all come together to make [the tour] an extension of who you are." From fireworks and pyrotechnic displays — sparks flew during opening number "Sparks Fly" — to acrobats twirling beneath giant bells, the Speak Now Tour was visually stunning, but it was hard for fans to take their eyes off Taylor giving her all every show: full of energy and full of gratitude that people bought tickets, came out to see her, and sang along to every song.

Hitting the stage in her favorite Roberto Cavalli dress, the Sparkly Wonder moved from "Sparks Fly" into "Mine" before modestly introducing herself to the audience: "My name is Taylor." With dancers and bandmates playing characters in the songs' stories, Taylor moved from a Depression-era small town for "Our Song" and "Mean" to an otherworldly fantasy forest for "Back to December," which she performed in a stunning Marchesa ballgown. The tour's title track got a full white wedding treatment with Taylor stealing the groom in a perky purple halter dress and ponytail, before she moved through the crowd to the B stage for stripped-down acoustic numbers. Other highlights included an emotional performance of "Dear John" that climaxed with the line "I'm shining like fireworks over your sad, empty town" with literal fireworks exploding from the stage to punctuate Taylor's triumph over this heartbreak.

In an interview with *20/20*, she told Katie Couric, "Going through these performances it's like an athletic marathon. When I'm underneath the stage and then it pops me up like a toaster [for "Our Song"] and then I'm like six feet in the air, and I'm like, 'Made it through that, did the banjo song, okay on to this next blocking, change clothes, flying above the crowd — awesome — coming out of a bell.' You just kind of get into a cycle of it; it's fun."

Even though a huge tour like this requires a certain degree of scripting and choreography, Taylor didn't want the show to get monotonous. "One of my favorite things about this tour — although it's a very theatrical show, and it really reminds me a lot of my favorite musical theater productions in its scenery, costumes, and production — there are a lot of moments in the show that are very spontaneous." On the B stage at the other end of the arena from the main stage, Taylor performed a different cover song every night, usually by a local artist. "It's been fun to be able to vary the show so much, especially because you'll have a lot of people who will come to more than one show, and I want them to get a different experience every time."

Some nights, Taylor had a little help singing those cover songs. The list of guests who popped up on the main stage with Taylor is a who's who of music — including Selena Gomez, Hayley Williams, Usher, T.I., B.o.B., Shawn Colvin, Nelly, Flo Rida, Kenny Chesney, Darius Rucker, Jason Mraz, Hot Chelle Rae, Justin Bieber, and, in a moment where Taylor sang with the man she was named after, James Taylor at Madison Square Garden performing "Fire and Rain" and then Taylor's own "Fifteen."

Taylor and Mr. Taylor had first met a few years earlier. Explained the legendary singer-songwriter, "She and I did a benefit together before she took off. We met then; her parents had played her a lot of my music when she was growing up and her mother told Taylor she named her after me. It was lovely to meet her and she seemed like a nice, young, earnest person trying to find her way in the music business. [Since then] she hasn't changed much — her circumstances have changed and she's handling it quite well." James Taylor invited Ms. Swift to join him onstage during his performance at Tanglewood in Massachusetts, and the younger Taylor happily obliged; the two sang "Fire and Rain," "Ours," and "Love Story." "I loved her songs," praised James, "and her presence on stage was so great."

On the other end of the musical spectrum, Taylor brought Nicki Minaj out to sing "Super Bass" at a stop at the Staples Center in Los Angeles on August 29, 2011. That moment had a backstory to it that speaks volumes about

SPEAK NOW SET LIST

Re-live the sparkly goodness with the set list from the North American leg of the Speak Now Tour:

1. "Sparks Fly"
2. "Mine"
3. "The Story of Us"
4. "Our Song"
5. "Mean"
6. "Back to December"
7. "Better Than Revenge"
8. "Speak Now"
9. "Fearless"
10. "Last Kiss"
11. "You Belong with Me"
12. "Dear John"
13. "Enchanted"
14. "Haunted"
15. "Long Live"
16. "Fifteen"
17. "Love Story"

Taylor's new status as a tastemaker. Back in February, she had sung a verse of the song during a radio interview, saying she loved "Super Bass," which was not yet a single off the *Pink Friday* album. Thanks to Taylor's endorsement, the song and Nicki got a whole new level of exposure, and soon Taylor and pal Selena Gomez could be seen singing along during Nicki's performance of the hit at the 2011 American Music Awards. On stage with Nicki on the Speak Now Tour, Taylor enthusiastically danced, rapped, and sang along with the hip-hop star. At the end of the song, Nicki told the crowd, "Taylor started this 'Super Bass' frenzy and I want to thank her from the bottom of my heart. I love you dearly."

Of her many willing guest acts, Taylor said, "I'm just as shocked by it as all the fans are in the audience — the fact that they would spend their evening coming out and playing for free for my fans." But cover songs weren't the only way Taylor paid respect to other songwriters on the Speak Now Tour. Every night, fans knew to expect a different lyric written down her arm, which showcased the breadth of Taylor's musical interest from Faith Hill to Eminem, Ingrid Michaelson to The Beach Boys.

Taylor decided that the tour was something she wanted to capture both for the fans who couldn't make it to the show, and for herself: "Every single night I stand on that stage and it feels like it's the best crowd of the tour every night. They are so loud and emotional and so passionate, and these crowds that we've played for this year have been unlike any crowd we've played for on any other tour, and this show has been different than anything we've ever put on. I want to look back on this years from now and show it to my kids and my grandkids." *Speak Now: World Tour Live*, Taylor's first live album and concert performance video, was released on November 21, 2011. Taylor dedicated the live package to "the beautiful, wonderful people who were kind enough to grace me with their presence and company in the stands, seats, and rafters of this tour. To those incredible people, thank you for hanging out with me."

BURNING *RED*

Not long after *Speak Now* hit the shelves, Taylor started penning songs for her follow-up album. At first, she approached it the same way as her last effort, writing the songs solo and producing with Nathan Chapman. But as the dynamic duo worked on the title track in the studio, Big Machine CEO Scott Borchetta thought the song wasn't living up to its potential. Taylor and Chapman went back at it, but when they still hadn't nailed it, Borchetta suggested seeking out renowned pop producer Max Martin. Taylor liked the idea. The collaboration went so well, it encouraged her to reach out to others. "'Red' the song was a real turning point for *Red* the album," Taylor told *Billboard*. "When I wrote that song, my mind started wandering to all the places we could go. If I were to think outside the box enough, go in with different people, I could learn from [them] and have what they do rub off on me as well as have what I do rub off on them."

"Writing by myself became a comfort zone," Taylor confessed. "So with this one, I really wanted to push myself." That meant approaching new collaborators, producers, and writers whom Taylor had admired from afar. She reached out to people outside country music, which meant moving away from the pop-country fusion Taylor had made her own. "I'm trying to be as much of a sponge as possible," she told MTV. "You have to evolve and try new things and change, and that's what I've loved to do with this album."

Though Taylor owes much of her success to country audiences, Scott Borchetta didn't worry when his star experimented with other

genres. "She made a record the same way she listens to music. One of the things we talked about early on was, when it's country, run toward it. When it's rock, run toward it. When it's pop, run toward it. You've got creative license, I've got your back." Taylor hasn't been afraid to cover rock, pop, and rap in her concerts, and now her enthusiasm for other genres was seeping onto her record. Taylor told Katie Couric, "I've been influenced by every possible corner of an iPod."

Scott Borchetta and Taylor hit the red carpet for the 5th Annual ACM Honors.

Of course, when her lead single, "We Are Never Ever Getting Back Together," hit the airwaves sounding, according to one *Spin* reviewer, like "the best hit Kelly Clarkson never had," there was a lot of worry that Taylor had permanently put her country side out to pasture. But the genre-skipping songstress insisted her musical education was ongoing. "Over and over again, Nashville has seen me experiment and seen me come back again," she said. "And I think people mistake success for the opportunity to coast. Just because something does well doesn't mean you should try to duplicate it, just repeat it and put a different cover and label on the front. I'm 22 years old, and it would be wrong to assume I know all I need to know about songwriting and craft and structure and being in the studio." She'd also learned that she'd never please everybody, and people were all too eager to box her in. "Almost every time I put something out, there's the word 'too' put in front of what it is — too pop or too country or too rock. I had a song last year called 'Mean' . . . and I remember reading a few articles that said it was too bluegrass. So I kinda stopped worrying about it. I'd rather be too something than not enough something."

What emerged was an eclectic collection of songs, which Swifty likened to "a patchwork quilt." Explained Taylor, "I tried to operate from an emotional place. I made the emotion of the song a priority rather than asking, 'What should we do from a production standpoint?' or 'What works in this genre?' Instead it was 'What did that emotion feel like when I wrote the song?' And whatever the answer was determined what the track sounded like and what my vocals were supposed to sound like."

But despite the songs' sonic diversity, they were united by their theme or, perhaps, their color: red. Whether passion or heartbreak, joy or anger, Taylor was seeing red. In her album announcement web chat, Taylor explained, "They're all pretty much about the tumultuous, crazy, insane, intense, semi-toxic relationships

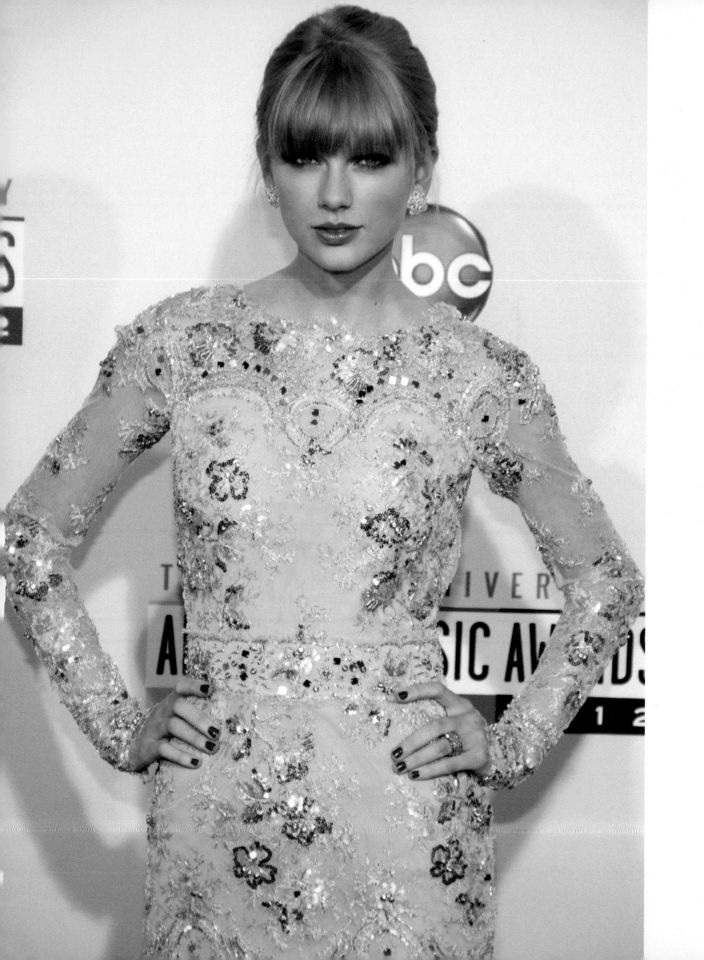

I've experienced in the last two years and all those emotions spanning from intense love, intense frustration, intense jealousy, confusion, all of that in my mind, all those emotions are red. There's nothing in between, there's nothing beige about those feelings."

Taylor was eager to share her new songs with fans and, returning to her strategy from *Speak Now*, used promotional singles to amp up the excitement for the album's release. This time she shared one new song per week on *Good Morning America* in the four weeks leading up to the day the album dropped. Each song shot to number one on the iTunes charts after its preview, and all made the top 15 on the Billboard Hot 100. (The highest-charting preview track? "I Knew You Were Trouble" hit number three.)

When the long-awaited October 22, 2012, release day arrived, fans poured into stores to get their hands on *Red*. But the album couldn't be found just anywhere, for Team Taylor had a bold business strategy: *Red* only appeared at retailers that wouldn't discount it deeply, in contrast to some albums (see: Lady Gaga's *Born This Way*) which are discounted to as low as 99 cents in an effort to boost first-week sales. Savvy partnerships meant *Red* was also available in some non-traditional outlets, like Papa John's Pizza, which splashed the singer all over their pizza boxes, had a special Taylor webpage, and a combo deal. Even though you could order an album with your pie, *Red* was conspicuously absent from streaming sites like Spotify. While these sites are often ways for listeners to warm up to new music, Taylor had millions of fans *paying* for the preview tracks she had pre-released; free streaming sites

seemed like a step back. The music industry still isn't sure whether live streaming sites cannibalize sales, and the megastar wasn't willing to risk it. It seems the strategy paid off: *Red* sold 1.21 million copies in its first week in the United States alone. Not only was this a personal record for Taylor, but the best first-week sales since Eminem's *The Eminem Show* in 2002. It was also the second-largest first week sales for a female artist *ever*, following Britney Spears' *Oops! . . . I Did It Again*. That first week, *Red* sold 2.12 million copies worldwide. The album took the top spot on the Billboard 200, holding it for three weeks (and landing back at the top at the end of 2012), as well as the top spot on the Country Albums list.

Overall, *Red* was a hit with the critics. *Rolling Stone* called it a "16-song geyser of willful eclecticism" and concluded, "her self-discovery project is one of the best stories in pop. When she's really on, her songs are like tattoos." *Billboard* praised, "*Red* puts Swift the artist front and center with big, beefy hooks that transcend her country roots for a genre-spanning record that reaches heights unseen since Shania Twain's *Up!*" The U.K.'s *Guardian* noted, "It's clear that *Red* is another chapter in one of the finest fantasies pop music has ever constructed." Some reviews were less effusive — the *L.A. Times* declared, "*Red* is a big record that reaches for Importance and occasionally touches it, filled with well-constructed pop songs Taylor-made for bedroom duets" and the *New York Times* decided, "Though often great, it is her least steady album, with some of her most sheer songwriting" — but all found something praiseworthy in the album's many shades of red.

CHAPTER 12

RED
SWIFT NOTES

1. "STATE OF GRACE"

BEHIND THE MUSIC Taylor noted that this track was one of the early songs that helped shape the album. She pinpointed one couplet in its chorus as defining the whole record: "Love is a ruthless game / Unless you play it good and right."

BETWEEN THE LINES In Christianity, a state of grace is that of divine forgiveness and unconditional love. This opening track presents two imperfect people (the Christian undertones continue with one being "not a saint") who find redemption, not in God's love, but in one another. And that love, while soaring and surprising, is not guaranteed or everlasting, which is perhaps why Taylor calls this song a warning. *Red* is an album of extremes of passion and heartbreak, and both are evident in its first song. The songwriter conjures a "golden age" but, sticking to classical references, also mentions an Achilles heel. In the instrumentation, she went for "a really big sound" that evokes "the feeling of falling in love in an epic way," but that grand romance is always edged by risk.

AUDIENCE OF ONE The references to "twin fire signs" and "four blue eyes" point to Jake Gyllenhaal, but the very private actor has kept his thoughts about this song (and the others likely about him) out of the papers.

FUN FACTS "Never" and "ever" are repeated over and over in this song — perhaps connecting it to the breakup anthem that seems to be for the same suitor.

DIARY DECODER If optimism dominates the song's lyrics, the secret message plays up that ever-present threat: "Love doesn't count after goodbye."

CHARTING SUCCESS The fourth promotional single for *Red*, "State of Grace," peaked at number 13 on the Hot 100.

2. "RED"

BEHIND THE MUSIC "Red" was a tough track to get right, and, rare for Taylor, it sat unfinished for months until the album's pop leanings clarified the song's sound.

BETWEEN THE LINES "Red" explores passion and pain as colors. Red alone can symbolize a huge range of emotion, as Taylor has pointed out, and perhaps the color's most defining characteristic is its intensity. The songwriter explained, "I wrote this song about the fact that some things are just hard to forget because the emotions involved with them were so intense and, to me, intense emotion is red."

FUN FACTS The chorus features a bouzouki, a Greek stringed instrument that sounds like a bass mandolin. A Maserati, an Italian luxury car, costs around $130,000. Drive carefully.

DIARY DECODER "SAG" could be another reference to the astrological sign that Jake and Taylor share (Sagittarius), although some point out it's also the acronym for Screen Actors Guild, of which Jake is an award-nominated member.

CHARTING SUCCESS "Red" climbed to number two on the U.S. Country Songs chart and number six on the Hot 100 chart.

3. "TREACHEROUS"

BEHIND THE MUSIC In a session with Dan Wilson, Taylor said she wanted to write a song around the word "treacherous." She suggested a melody, and the song exploded from there. Wilson told *Billboard*, "We thought we were done, and then we decided it needed a more rocking element, so we added [another] chorus after the chorus. It was almost an afterthought, but the new section wound up defining the song."

BETWEEN THE LINES "Treacherous" is a defiantly sensual song — from the physical descriptions in the lyrics to the sultry whisper of the verses. It revels in present pleasure, celebrating moments of unshakeable connection regardless of consequences. Taylor confessed to *USA Today* that song was about a relationship she knew "would end in fiery, burning wreckage." But, she noted, "There's something about that magnetic draw that doesn't really let up. You walk toward it anyway."

FUN FACTS Taylor called on Semisonic frontman Dan Wilson to help write this song. Wilson has had great success with other songwriting collaborations, such as Adele's number-one superhit "Someone Like You." Wilson praised Taylor: "An interesting quality, objectively speaking, was how on fire she was, the clarity she had. She was so open and excited about the things I would add. She works at a very high level of positivity, and that is rare."

DIARY DECODER "Won't stop til it's over" echoes the song's message that sometimes you have to hang on to something good as long as you can.

4. "I KNEW YOU WERE TROUBLE"

BEHIND THE MUSIC Taylor got the idea for this song almost six months before she was scheduled to write with Max Martin, so she emailed him saying how excited she was. She set out the melody for the chorus on the piano and, when the writing date finally arrived, brought her composition to Martin and his frequent

According to Scott Borchetta, Justin Bieber told Taylor that he thinks "I Knew You Were Trouble" "is the best song ever" and declared he'd make his next lip sync video of it. But Selena Gomez, Taylor's dear friend, managed to one-up him without even trying, posting a video of her and some friends doing a choreographed routine to the song on the Swift One's 23rd birthday.

DIARY DECODER "When you saw me dancing" could have been a first encounter, but it's a hotly debated topic as to who cast his eyes on Taylor.

CHARTING SUCCESS This third single shot to number three on the Hot 100. According to ABC News, "I Knew You Were Trouble" marked Taylor's 50th Hot 100 single, landing her in the company of an elite group of female hit makers: Madonna, Aretha Franklin, Dionne Warwick, and Connie Francis. (Though Taylor hadn't released 50 official singles, her previews were included in that total.)

production collaborator Shellback, telling them, "At the end of the chorus, I just want this to go crazy. I want it to be really chaotic."

BETWEEN THE LINES "I Knew You Were Trouble" goes in new directions, sonically and lyrically. While this song resides soundly in the pop camp, it integrates R&B vocal influences and dance-hall rhythms, distortion, and dubstep. Her message is just as bold: rather than blaming the guy for being bad news, she takes it on herself, having ignored the warning signs. "It talks about that feeling of not 'shame on you, you broke my heart,' [but] 'shame on *me*, you broke my heart,'" explained Taylor.

5. "ALL TOO WELL"

BEHIND THE MUSIC The first written for the record, this song was also the hardest for Taylor to write, coming at the end of a six-month writer's block that stemmed from a particularly bad breakup. The songwriter told Katie Couric, "I was going through something that was so hard that it was almost stifling, and so I wrote all these verses about everything from beginning to end of this relationship, and it ended up being, like, a 10-minute song." This epic draft completed, Taylor called on her old songwriting pal Liz Rose to help her whittle it down to the essentials.

BETWEEN THE LINES "All Too Well" is far from the fairytale scenarios of Taylor's *Fearless* days, instead it's grounded in the details of real romance: a road trip sing-along, an impromptu dance in the kitchen, family reminiscences, and intimate keepsakes. These moments revisited make the song as vivid as its autumnal backdrop. For listeners, as for the songwriter, they're scenes not easily forgotten. "All Too Well" is both sweet and sorrowful, those memories made more precious by the fact that the relationship is over. "It's a really emotional song because it does show you why loss is so painful," said Taylor, "because it was once good and you can remember it."

AUDIENCE OF ONE There are plenty of hints that point to Jake Gyllenhaal: the fall romance, the visit to his sister's home in Brooklyn (where Taylor spent Thanksgiving 2010), his glasses-wearing youth, and the scarf that she was photographed wearing while dating him (and that makes an appearance in the "Never Ever" video).

(NOT SO) FUN FACTS When folk singer-songwriter Matt Nathanson noticed Taylor's line "and I forget about you long enough to forget why I needed to" matched one from his song "I Saw" in everything but verb tense, he tweeted, "She's definitely a fan . . . and now she's a thief." Taylor has covered his songs in concert and written his lyrics on her arm. It might have been an accident or a coincidence, but Taylor's reps didn't comment.

DIARY DECODER Ever since Taylor and Jake were heavily photographed drinking "maple lattes" on a date, the festive fall beverages have been associated with them.

6. "22"

BEHIND THE MUSIC Sitting on a plane, Taylor got the idea for a song that would celebrate her summer: a time when she got to stay put for a while, recording her album from nine to five, then savoring being gloriously 22 with her pals.

BETWEEN THE LINES As in "Fifteen," at the age celebrated in "22" there is still heartbreak and bad choices and great friends, but rather than looking ahead as she did as a high schooler, she's realizes she's living something worthy of a euphoric dance floor anthem. "For me, being 22 has been my favorite year of my life," said Taylor. "I like all the possibilities of how you're still learning, but you know enough. You still know nothing, but you know that you know nothing. You're old enough to start planning your life, but you're young enough to know there are so many unanswered questions. That brings about a carefree feeling that is sort of based on indecision and fear and, at the same time, letting loose. Being 22 has taught me so much."

FUN FACTS Asked about the producer she worked with on this irresistible pop song, Taylor had nothing but praise: "I have always been so fascinated by how Max Martin can just land a chorus. He comes at you and hits you and it's a chorus — all caps, with exclamation points."

DIARY DECODER This one's for some of Taylor's buds: "Ashley" (Avignone), "Dianna" (Agron), "Claire" (Kislinger), and "Selena" (Gomez).

7. "I ALMOST DO"

BEHIND THE MUSIC This song emerged in a moment just like the one described in the

RED: THE DELUXE EDITION

At 16 songs, *Red* has the most cuts of a Taylor album to date, and yet she still was saddened to see how many were left off. Once again, she managed to slip in a few extras by way of the deluxe edition. Taylor said, "If I had been allowed to put 19 tracks on the record, I would have put these three songs that I wanted so badly to be on the album, and the fact that I get to share them with fans anyway feels so great." As with *Speak Now*, the deluxe edition was initially only in store at Target and online on iTunes.

Like Taylor's previous deluxe offering, *Red* offers three new songs and three alternate versions of the album's tracks. "The Moment I Knew" is the sorrowful tale of Taylor's 21st birthday, which despite a Christmas theme and good friends, took a sad turn when her boyfriend (hint: his name rhymes with "snake") didn't show up, and she realized her romance had fizzled. The songwriter has called it "the worst birthday party I ever had" and noted that a breakup soon followed. "Come Back . . . Be Here" is a second offering from Taylor's collaboration with Semisonic frontman Dan Wilson, describing a romance that seems doomed by distance; there aren't any hints as to whether or not this relationship passed the two-day mark described. A serial flirter is taken to task in the jaunty "Girl at Home." Discussing the song's subject, Taylor noted, "I just felt like it was disgusting that he was flirting with other girls." Taylor gives listeners a glimpse inside the studio with original demos of "Treacherous" and "Red," and rounds out bonus material with a heartbreaking acoustic rendition of "State of Grace." "It's really sweet and slowed down and it completely changes the song," said Taylor.

song, and Taylor needed a distraction: "Writing the song was what I did instead of picking up the phone."

BETWEEN THE LINES The lone acoustic guitar sets the tone for the longing of this song. "I Almost Do" occupies the place between total heartbreak and healing, when reuniting almost seems possible, but, as Taylor points out, rekindling an already failed romance means a high risk of going through all the pain anew. "'I Almost Do' is a song I wrote about the conflict that you feel when you want to take someone back, and you want to give it another try, but you know you can't," said Taylor. "And you can't because it's hurt you so deeply that you know you couldn't bear to go through that again."

DIARY DECODER "Wrote this instead of calling" makes the song feel even more honest, written as it was in the actual moment Taylor felt everything in the song.

8. "WE ARE NEVER EVER GETTING BACK TOGETHER"

BEHIND THE MUSIC Taylor was in the studio working on another song with Max Martin and Shellback, when a friend of her ex walked in and said he'd heard the two lovers were making up. When he left, Taylor went on a rant, telling her producers they were never ever getting back together. Like, ever. Max saw a song there, and they started writing. "It came from a very real place and it came from a very spontaneous situation," she said. Taylor started strumming the guitar and calling the chorus, then asked, "Is that too obvious? Is that too obvious to just say that over and over again?" The producers didn't think so, and 25 minutes later, they had a song.

BETWEEN THE LINES "Never Ever" is an intuitive track to follow the indecision and wistfulness of "I Almost Do." By the time this infectious pop earworm kicks in, she's made up her mind and comes off as confident, triumphant, and even . . . happy. Taylor called this "a breakup song in the form of a parade." Though it could seem like a throwaway detail, Taylor has called the indie records line the most important in the song. "It was a relationship where I felt very critiqued and subpar," she said. "He'd listen to this music that nobody had heard of . . . but as soon as anyone else liked these bands, he'd drop them. I felt that was a strange way to be a music fan." Her best revenge for that judgment? Crafting an international pop hit he'd hear everywhere he went: "I made a song that I knew would absolutely drive him crazy when he heard it on the radio. Not only would it hopefully be played a lot, so that he'd have to hear it, but it's the opposite of the kind of music that he was trying to make me feel inferior to."

AUDIENCE OF ONE Looks like Jake Gyllenhaal is the indie music snob in question here. Fans connected the scarf in the "Never Ever" video with Taylor's serial scarf wearing during her relationship with Gyllenhaal. When Katie Couric asked about it, Taylor replied, "I didn't know that that was a thing that people figured out."

DIARY DECODER "When I stopped caring what you thought" highlights the defiant freedom of this track.

CHARTING SUCCESS "Never Ever" was Taylor's first song to top the Billboard Hot 100. Swifty called the chart triumph "a serious jumping-up-and-down-screaming moment." It also broke the record for highest weekly digital sales for a female performer with 623,000 downloads in the first week and climbed to the top of the iTunes charts in 32 countries. Just over two months after its release, "Never Ever" earned its double platinum certification. The song also nabbed a Grammy nomination for Record of the Year.

9. "STAY STAY STAY"

BEHIND THE MUSIC Keeping that same mix of good-spirited pep and digs at ex-boyfriends from the previous track, Taylor penned a song that celebrates the little moments — good and bad — that make up a relationship.

BETWEEN THE LINES If "Never Ever" makes breaking up almost seem fun, "Stay Stay Stay" skips in to remind listeners that sometimes it can be worth hanging in there. Plucky and earnest, it shifts away from the slick pop of the last song and back to her pop-country roots. Despite the opening fight, "Stay Stay Stay" depicts quite a peaceful relationship compared to the other roller coasters on the album. Taylor said the song is "based on what I've seen of real relationships, where it's not perfect, there are moments where you're just so sick of that person and you get into a stupid fight, [but] it's still worth it to stay in it, because there's something about it that you can't live without."

FUN FACTS *American Songwriter* highlighted this track as one on the album that showcases how "phenomenally good at capturing those moments in tangible detail" Taylor Swift is in her songwriting.

DIARY DECODER "Daydreaming about real love" implies this one's not based on Taylor's personal experience.

10. "THE LAST TIME"

BEHIND THE MUSIC In this case, one duet led to another. Taylor was in the studio with Ed Sheeran recording "Everything Has Changed," when Ed told her he'd like her to meet his friend Gary Lightbody. A huge Snow Patrol fan, she eagerly agreed, and when Gary heard their work, he wanted to write for her record. The two met at producer Jacknife Lee's house, where Gary played a melody that gave Taylor an idea for the narrative for the song.

BETWEEN THE LINES "The Last Time" is an interesting first for a Taylor Swift album: not only is it the first male-female duet, but a male's perspective is represented. With the audible regret in his delivery, this serial heartbreaker becomes a bit sympathetic. It's a deliberately repetitive song to underscore the fact that this conversation is a routine for the couple. Taylor

had a strong image in her mind while composing this tale: a guy standing outside the door in the cold, asking for *another* second chance, and a girl knowing she can't give him one. Taylor told NPR's *All Things Considered*, "The idea was based on this experience that I had with someone who was this unreliable guy, you never know when he's going to leave or when he's going to come back, but he always comes back."

FUN FACTS Gary's band Snow Patrol went five times platinum with their major label debut, *Final Straw*, and got the world's attention with their follow-up album, *Eyes Open*. Jacknife Lee, the producer on this song, has also worked with legendary bands like U2 and R.E.M.

DIARY DECODER "LA on your break" points to Jake (who takes breaks between films) or John Mayer (who takes breaks between tours).

11. "HOLY GROUND"

BEHIND THE MUSIC After Taylor ran into an ex, she was thinking about their past together and said to herself, "You know what? That was good . . . having that in my life." From that encounter and the feeling it left her with came "Holy Ground."

BETWEEN THE LINES Carried along with insistent drums, "Holy Ground" is a surprisingly upbeat song about lost happy days. It dances on details, sweeping through the early days of a new relationship. Taylor described it as "a song I wrote about the feeling I got after years had gone by, and I finally appreciated a past relationship for what it was, rather than being bitter about what it didn't end up being."

AUDIENCE OF ONE If this is a song about Joe Jonas, as many fans theorize, it marks a big step in the evolution of Taylor's feelings about her ex, which began with a mix of anger and sadness in "Forever & Always," moved through sorrow in "Last Kiss," and here with "Holy Ground" into appreciation.

FUN FACTS For this track, Taylor sought out producer Jeff Bhasker, who has worked with artists like Kanye West, fun., Beyoncé, Alicia Keys, and kid cudi.

DIARY DECODER Joe Jonas and Taylor Lautner are the only Taylor exes who still attend her shows, so it looks like "When you came to the show in SD" is directed at one of them.

12. "SAD BEAUTIFUL TRAGIC"

BEHIND THE MUSIC Taylor got out her guitar and composed this one on a tour bus, letting the rhymes of the chorus lead the way. When she got home, she asked Nathan Chapman to record that same day. He agreed, and the vocals from the original demo were used on the album, because that first cut "came across so pure and raw," according to Taylor.

BETWEEN THE LINES Though it may have been a beautiful affair, in this song we only see the end of it. "Sad Beautiful Tragic" barely raises itself above a whisper, as if the relationship is too sacred, and its dissolution too devastating, to do otherwise. The songwriter told *Billboard*, "I wanted to tell the story in terms of a cloudy recollection of what went wrong. It's kind of the murky gray, looking back on something you can't change or get back."

DIARY DECODER "While you were on a train" could refer to Gyllenhaal, who filmed *Source Code*, a movie set in large part on a train, while the pair was dating. He also rode a train with Mumford & Sons on their Railroad Revival

Tour in 2011. (The rail trip was months after their breakup, but their relationship seems to have been a hard one for Taylor to get over.)

13. "THE LUCKY ONE"

BEHIND THE MUSIC This one was written on the road in the land down under.

BETWEEN THE LINES Though Taylor never complains about the pressures and perils of being

Ed Sheeran had "RED" added to his sleeve tattoo after the announcement was made that he'd be joining Taylor on her tour.

of." Chief among those fears are no longer having fun with her career, and of feeling hollow and misunderstood while being heralded as a golden girl. She admitted to the *Tennessean*, "I'm fearful of people getting tired of me, or fearful of my life ending up a cliché of a person who has people around them all the time but in what matters most they're alone."

AUDIENCE OF ONE This could be as simple as Taylor singing about her fears, or the details of this track could point to Joni Mitchell. Joni was "a sixties queen" with a "made up name" (she was born Roberta Joan Anderson) in Los Angeles. Going deeper, the title track of Mitchell's 1972 album, *For the Roses*, expresses her fatigue with the music business, and she took a break after that record's release, much like the subject of Taylor's song who "chose the rose garden over Madison Square." Unlike the disenchanted star in the song, Mitchell returned to the business, releasing one of her biggest hits, *Court and Spark*, in 1974, and many more albums over the next 40 years.

FUN FACTS This song has a lot in common with a track by another artist Taylor admires: Britney Spears' "Lucky."

DIARY DECODER Could "Wouldn't you like to know" be a knowing joke about the scrutiny Taylor's songs provoke about her life?

14. "EVERYTHING HAS CHANGED"

BEHIND THE MUSIC Taylor's first exposure to Ed Sheeran came when she saw his "Lego House" video while touring Australia. She recalled, "I fell in love with his music and I couldn't believe we hadn't had his album come out in the U.S. yet. So I reached out to his manage-

in the spotlight, this ballad reveals she does worry about it sometimes. She explained, "I'm pretty much singing about what I'm scared ment to see if he wanted to write, but at the same time he was reaching out to my management as well. So it was very strange." Once they worked it out, Ed flew to L.A., where they settled onto a trampoline in Swift's backyard to write, passing a guitar between them. He started singing harmony with Taylor, which sparked the idea of a duet. And, Taylor added, "For portions of the song, [we were bouncing around] 'cause it's a trampoline and it's fun, and the combined maturity level of both of us is eight years old."

BETWEEN THE LINES This romantic duet teases out all the enticing possibility of a new beginning. Taylor explained, "It's about meeting someone and all of a sudden your entire perspective on the world changes — you're thinking for two, instead of one."

AUDIENCE OF ONE Given the coded hint in the album booklet and Conor Kennedy's green eyes, it's likely this one's for him.

FUN FACTS Ed Sheeran is a British singer-songwriter whose debut album, +, went four times platinum in the U.K. Production credits on this song go to Butch Walker, a singer-songwriter and producer who has worked behind the board with Katy Perry, Dashboard Confessional, Pink, Weezer, and many more. Walker is slightly less well known for his impromptu cover of "You Belong with Me" that caused Taylor to comment, "I'm losing my MIND listening to it! Blown away."

DIARY DECODER "Hyiannis Port" (or, spelled correctly, Hyannis Port) is where the Kennedys have their compound, and where Conor Kennedy and Taylor were photographed on a series of dates over the summer of 2012.

Says Ethel Kennedy of Taylor, "She's very kind and . . . do you know what she really is? She's game. She had never sailed before. She sailed. She had never gone dragging before, she dragged. She played everything that everyone else was doing and she was good at it. And [with] no fuss."

15. "STARLIGHT"

BEHIND THE MUSIC A photo of Ethel and Robert F. Kennedy at a dance in the late '40s was the inspiration for this song. Taylor came across it while looking at old photos for fashion ideas, and thought, "They look like they're having the best night." Taylor told the *Wall Street Journal*, "So I just kind of wrote that song from that place, not really knowing how they met or anything like that."

BETWEEN THE LINES This enchanting number starts with a twinkling intro that itself seems made of starlight, then sweeps the listener onto the dance floor as the chorus kicks in — a dynamic that musically mimics what it's like to fall in love. "Starlight" takes two members of American royalty and casts them as teens falling in love, skipping rocks and sneaking into parties. It's a familiar Taylor tactic, and one that keeps her relatable even when her charmed life is the farthest thing from an average existence.

AUDIENCE OF ONE Taylor met one of the famous subjects of her song after Ethel's daughter Rory came to a Taylor Swift show and, hearing about the song, invited the songwriter to meet her mom. Ethel "just loved" the song, according to Taylor. Ethel has effusively and publicly praised Taylor, telling *People*, "She's just sensational inside and out."

FUN FACTS Taylor was honored by the Kennedy clan at their December 2012 Ripple of Hope Gala for the Robert F. Kennedy Center for Justice and Human Rights where she performed this song.

DIARY DECODER This one's a dedication Taylor doesn't feel the need to hide: "For Ethel."

16. "BEGIN AGAIN"

BETWEEN THE LINES After her lead single from *Red* suggested a defection to the pop camp, "Begin Again" was a reassuring second release for country fans, for this soft, sweet ballad complete with banjo and plaintive fiddle is classic Taylor Swift. In the opening scene, Taylor is vulnerable as she reassesses what she likes, trying to free it from the taint of a disapproving boyfriend. When a new guy arrives on the scene, he bolsters her flagging confidence, reminding her she's funny and has great taste. For Taylor, once she's through the worst of the breakup, there's a part of her open to that new beginning. "Even after [a relationship] explodes into a million pieces and burns down and you're standing in a pile of the ash of what it once was, thinking, 'Why did I have to meet this person, why did this have to happen?'" Taylor explained to *Marie Claire*. "But then, when you make eye contact with someone across the room and it clicks and, bam, you're there. In love again."

AUDIENCE OF ONE Taylor has said the first and the last songs on the record are about the same person, bookending it with the beginning of that relationship and moving on from it. All signs point to Jake for the heartbreak, but the new love is a little less clear. Conor Kennedy and Parachute frontman Will Anderson have both been put forward as candidates.

FUN FACTS Katy Perry declared "Begin Again" one of her favorite songs of 2012.

DIARY DECODER "I wear heels now" seems to be directed toward Jake Gyllenhaal, her only ex who would be dwarfed by the 5'11" singer when she wore heels.

CHARTING SUCCESS The second single from *Red* shot to the top of the Hot Digital Songs chart and made it to number four on the Hot 100.

CHAPTER 13

LOVE STORIES

TAYLOR'S VIDEOS

"TIM McGRAW"

THE CONCEPT Taylor's first music video follows the song's lyrics very faithfully. In a scene that's almost too beautiful to be real, Taylor lays beside a lake as evening approaches. She's holding a radio and singing to her departed boyfriend. While the boyfriend is driving away, he hears a song on his truck's radio that makes him turn back. Between those scenes are flashes of the memories that the Tim McGraw song brings back — horsing around in a field, lying in a pickup truck and looking at the stars, and, of course, slow dancing all night long.

GUEST STARRING Clayton Collins was cast because he looked like the guy Taylor wrote the song for.

FUN FACTS "Tim McGraw" was directed by Trey Fanjoy, who went on to direct five more of Taylor's videos. Trey has also made award-nominated videos with Reba McEntire, George Strait, and Miranda Lambert.

DID YOU NOTICE? The truck in the video is a Chevy (but it doesn't get stuck as it does in the lyrics). The bracelet Taylor's wearing in the bed of the truck reads "Live In Love." The letter wedged in the cabin door is for "Johnny"; that name was used because that cabin once belonged to country music legend Johnny Cash. While the outside of it looks rustic, the inside has been (appropriately) transformed into a recording studio.

"TEARDROPS ON MY GUITAR"

THE CONCEPT Fans are familiar with the story behind this song, and the video lays it out well. Taylor's got a crush on Drew, who's unfortunately smitten with another girl. The video alternates between the great times the pair spends together at school and Taylor alone on her bed with only her guitar and those memories for company. Taylor returned to high school, Hume-Fogg High in downtown Nashville, to film this video, an experience she called "a little strange, but in a good way."

GUEST STARRING Tyler Hilton, a talented actor and musician, plays Drew. He's best known as Chris Keller on the CW's *One Tree Hill* and for playing young Elvis Presley in *Walk the Line*. Taylor happened to read a magazine article where Tyler mentioned being a fan of her music. She invited him to a show, and then offered him the role in the "Teardrops" music video. "He's such a great actor and he brought out a lot in me. You know, because I'm not an actor," said Taylor. "He was really, really cool and it was good to have the chance to become friends with him. He's a sweetheart." Since they didn't want a high school with empty halls, Taylor got to cast some of her friends as extras! Abigail, Kathryn, Kelsey, Ally, Emily, Megan, bro Austin, and her cousin all make an appearance.

FUN FACTS The aquamarine gown Taylor wears was custom made by stylist Sandi Spika Borchetta, wife of Scott Borchetta, and the dress measures 21 feet long. Taylor managed to wear it on the red carpet of the 2007 CMT Music Awards!

DID YOU NOTICE? On the fireplace mantle is the Latin phrase *litera scripta manet*. It means "the written word endures," which is one of the reasons Taylor writes songs — to capture her experiences so she won't ever forget them.

In her gown from the "Teardrops" video, Taylor poses with her CMT Music Award on April 16, 2007.

"OUR SONG"

THE CONCEPT Unlike most of Taylor's videos, "Our Song" doesn't tell a story, instead it lets vibrant colors and symbols of romance do the talking. Trey Fanjoy, who'd directed Taylor's first two videos, dreamed up the concept. The video star related, "When [Trey] heard the song, she had this idea for a front porch performance and then a field of flowers for another performance, then a black-and-white performance shot. It all came together in her head. She was able to translate that so well

Video director Trey Fanjoy, Taylor, stylist Sandy Spika Borchetta, and Big Machine Records' Scott Borchetta embrace backstage at the 2008 CMT Awards.

onto film. It just shows what a truly great director she is."

GUEST STARRING The only guest stars in this video are Taylor's band, who make their first video appearance.

FUN FACTS This is the first video that features "Sparkles," Taylor's trademark guitar. Taylor had two dresses custom made for this shoot.

DID YOU NOTICE? Taylor has a heart on her foot just like in the album booklet (though on the other foot). Even though she said she'd get it permanently tattooed if her first album went double platinum, her dad changed her mind, jokingly threatening he'd take it off with a belt sander! Also, while Taylor's getting ready at the beginning of the video her hair is straight but when she emerges from the house she's got her trademark curls.

"PICTURE TO BURN"

THE CONCEPT The "Picture to Burn" video starts with Abigail and Taylor parked outside Taylor's ex-boyfriend's place spying on him. Seeing him with another girl (driving his pickup truck!), Taylor has an elaborate revenge fantasy. Taylor joked to CMT, "The storyline of the video is if you break up with me, my band will ransack your house."

GUEST STARRING The video's bad boy is played by former Tennessee Titans football player Justin Sandy who was a little apprehensive about his villainous role. "I'm gonna have every girl in the United States hate me after this video," he joked. Justin was selected because, according to Taylor, "We wanted him to be classically, like, almost too cute." Abigail Anderson plays a true-to-life role — Taylor's BFF. This was her second time in one of Taylor's videos, but only the back of her head was visible in "Teardrops on My Guitar." Taylor's band members are back, this time with juicy roles as her agents of revenge. "They have the most hilarious sense of humor and I really wanted to portray that in this video," said Taylor. Describing the shoot, Taylor wrote, "My band was in the video a lot, and they were wearing these amazing black business suits and aviators. They looked like secret agents. Except with more highlights." After that shoot, they started referring to themselves as "The Agency."

FUN FACTS Day one of this video, also known as "pyro day," was shot in the same arena where they film the CMA Awards. Before filming the fire-heavy scenes, Taylor was a little bit nervous about her first pyrotechnic experience, confessing, "There are some things I'm nervous about. My hair could very well catch on fire."

DID YOU NOTICE? The video uses the radio edit of the song, not the album version.

"LOVE STORY"

THE CONCEPT Taylor spies her Romeo while walking out of school, and it seems like the two knew each other in another lifetime. Scenes of an elaborate *Romeo and Juliet* fantasy alternate between Taylor waiting for her Romeo in a castle and the couple's story — meeting at a party, sneaking out to meet at night in a garden, and finally, coming together in the field (a scene that Taylor always dreamed of shooting).

GUEST STARRING Taylor searched for six months to find the right person, before picking Justin Gaston because he "looked very timeless." The model (and one-time close friend of Miley Cyrus) reprised his role as Romeo at the 2008 CMAs when Taylor performed "Love Story." A singer himself, Justin competed on season six of the reality show *Nashville Star* and also appears in the *Glee* pilot.

FUN FACTS Though the 20 dancers in the party scene are professionals, Taylor had to learn the ballroom dance in 15 minutes! Taylor's two gowns were specially designed for her over a two month period by stylist Sandi Spika Borchetta, who had Taylor's input every step of the way. The video was shot during a heat wave, which felt even hotter for Taylor with tights, a corset, and a heavy dress on. The corset was a bigger challenge than the heat.

Justin Gaston joins Taylor onstage as she performs "Love Story" at the 2008 CMAs.

"You've got, like, a 20-minute period when you're not feeling like your lungs are going to collapse, and after that you're pretty much on your deathbed," said Taylor. While shooting this video, Taylor found out she was nominated for a Teen Choice Award for Choice Breakout Artist.

DID YOU NOTICE? The sun is quite a bit lower

when Taylor runs to her Romeo in the field than "seconds" before when she's waiting in the castle. That's because the field wasn't actually in front of the castle. The castle scenes were shot at Castle Gwynn in Arrington-Triune, Tennessee, and the field was a car-ride away, which meant the crew raced to finish filming the field scene before sunset.

"WHITE HORSE"

THE CONCEPT In this moody video, Taylor cries alone in a dark room, remembering both the good times she had with her ex and the worst moment — when she found out that he had another girlfriend. In the end, she decides he doesn't deserve a second chance. Taylor explained, "It's not really another 'guy cheats on me' video. You find out that I'm kind of the one that's kinda ruining the relationship without even knowing it." Once again directed by Trey Fanjoy, "White Horse" was a departure from her earlier videos. "This video is a lot different than the other videos that we've made, 'cause usually we've gone for bright colors and me looking straight to camera and singing. [This video is] a little more introspective," said Taylor.

GUEST STARRING The heartbreaker-du-jour in "White Horse" is Stephen Colletti, best known for *Laguna Beach* and *One Tree Hill*. Explaining her choice, Taylor noted, "He had sort of the look we were going for . . . because the guy in the video is supposed to look really sweet and someone who just looks like he would never lie to you. But in the video, he does."

DID YOU NOTICE? During her crying scene, there are two horse figurines in the room with Taylor — one on the amp beside her and one on the mantle. The restaurant scene was shot at the Mad Platter in Nashville.

"YOU BELONG WITH ME"

THE CONCEPT Taylor's got a split personality in this video, playing both the mean girl brunette cheerleader and the literal girl-next-door, who are competing for the attention of the high school football star. The leading man and Taylor exchange proto text messages through their bedroom windows, but it's not until a made-over Taylor appears at prom that they have the courage to share their "I love you" notes.

GUEST STARRING Lucas Till plays the hunk-next-door; he's best known for playing Miley's flame in *Hannah Montana: The Movie*. There's another guest star in this video who is less recognizable: Taylor's body double, Kelly, who helped out with those scenes where Taylor had to be in two places at once. "You Belong with Me" also saw Taylor's band suit up and join the action once again, this time as fellow band geeks.

FUN FACTS "You Belong with Me" was shot at Pope John Paul II High School in Hendersonville where lil' bro Austin Swift was a student. The high school supplied some prom-goers (their actual prom was the night after the shoot) and helped fill the bleachers at the football game. The "Junior Jewels" T-shirt Taylor is wearing is a loaner from Caitlin Evanson, Taylor's fiddler. It's signed by Caitlin's band camp friends. It's also a popular do-it-yourself costume for fans attending Taylor's concerts. The periodic table shirt? That's Taylor's own contribution to the wardrobe. Director Roman White was thrilled

Lucas Till admitted that he was "crushing on Taylor for a while," so he must have been thrilled to play the object of her affection in "You Belong with Me."

She walked differently. She spoke differently. She even had some fantastic new evil looks she'd toss around. It was GREAT!"

DID YOU NOTICE? Even though Taylor's wearing giant glasses, she's the one who can see clearly in this video. Taylor needs prescription lenses in real life, though she usually opts for contacts over her black square-framed eyewear.

"FIFTEEN"

THE CONCEPT Most of "Fifteen" takes place in a sort of dream world as Taylor looks back on her high school years. Director Roman White, who also directed "You Belong with Me," explained, "I wanted to do something different from what Taylor had done before. We wanted to take this one outside of high school. The idea is that there's a place where you can go back and revisit your memories. She's in this void and memories are manifesting around her. The story evolves and she walks across this dream world. When she walks through those doors and people fade in and out, she just has this amazing sense of innocence." Taylor exits the dream world at the very end of the video when she stands outside the high school, watching the new girls who the advice in this song is for.

GUEST STARRING Abigail Anderson is becoming a regular in Taylor Swift videos, though this appearance is special, since she's named in the song and is the focus of the video for a verse.

FUN FACTS Almost the entire video was shot in front of a green screen, making it a real test of Taylor's acting abilities. About Nashville native Roman White, Taylor says, "He is hilarious. He is just walking around making jokes, cracking people up the entire time."

with Taylor's portrayal of the mean cheerleader: "I think Taylor had a blast playing two very different roles. The weirdest part was that she really CHANGED once that wig went on.

TAYLOR'S HOME VIDEOS

For three of her songs, Taylor didn't turn to the professionals, but dove into her own video footage to create something all her own.

"I'm Only Me When I'm with You" is a video Taylor edited herself as a gift to her fans while they waited for the "Picture to Burn" video to come out. It's full of candid shots, goofy driving moments, and intimate performance scenes. It showcases many of Taylor's loved ones including Kellie Pickler, Abigail Anderson, Faith Hill and Tim McGraw, the Swift family, her band, and an adorable orange kitten.

"Beautiful Eyes" was included on Taylor's 2008 EP, *Beautiful Eyes*. Featuring footage from her 18th birthday party, fans got a peek at the special video montage Taylor's parents made for her as well as clips of the birthday girl celebrating with her closest friends.

"The Best Day" video was a Christmas gift for her mother, Andrea. Taylor chose her footage carefully, with the pictures taking cues from the song. It's especially neat to hear Taylor sing, "There is a video I found from back when I was three / You set up a paint set in the kitchen and you're talking to me," and to see the actual video she's singing about.

DID YOU NOTICE? Taylor wears two white dresses in this video, bringing the number of white dresses she wears in her videos to six.

"FEARLESS"

THE CONCEPT The video is a whirlwind look at the Fearless Tour that combines key concert moments with backstage, rehearsal, and meet-and-greet footage and has an old-style film projector quality.

GUEST STARRING Beyond Taylor's Fearless Tour crew, her fans are the stars of this video featured in shots of her thrilled audiences and in footage of the signs, clothes, and jewelry fans make to celebrate their love of Taylor.

FUN FACTS The director of this video, Todd Cassetty, had worked with Taylor before; he put together the enhanced CD features for *Fearless: Platinum Edition.*

"MINE"

THE CONCEPT Taylor's character catches the eye of a cute waiter in a café, and a whole love story unfolds: we see their courtship, struggles, wedding, and family frolicking fun, as well as flashbacks to a young Taylor witnessing her parents' marital discord. Intercut with all those flashforwards and flashbacks are beautiful performance shots of Taylor in a whimsical forest where photographs hang from the trees. As for the ending back at the café, Taylor joked, "Was it a flashforward? Did it happen? Is it something she daydreamed happened? You don't know. None of us know . . . I don't even know."

GUEST STARRING British actor Toby Hemingway was handpicked by Taylor after she watched the movie *Feast of Love.* "I was doing some more research and watched another movie he

"CHANGE"

THE CONCEPT "Change" is Taylor's first performance-only video (meaning there's no storyline at all), but when NBC broadcast the video, it was spliced with clips of the 2008 U.S. Olympians who had stories all their own.

GUEST STARRING Taylor's band is back, doing what they do best.

FUN FACTS The video was shot at the Scottish Rite Cathedral in Indianapolis, Indiana.

was in called *The Covenant*," she said. "I've got this crazy 13 lucky thing, and he walks onscreen for the first time wearing a sweatshirt with a 13 on it! That was the deciding factor. It wasn't really up to me; it was about the number." Director Roman White was pleased with his star's choice of a leading man: "It's always fun having someone around who's British. It just makes everything sound cooler . . . He was great to work with."

When it came time to cast the children in the video, Taylor looked to Jaclyn Jarrett, daughter of professional wrestler Jeff Jarrett, to play the younger version of herself. Taylor knows the Jarrett family from Hendersonville, and she flew in Jaclyn and her two sisters as well as Kyra Angle to appear in the video. Taylor's role as casting director wasn't done yet: she and her mom spotted a three-year-old boy, Liam, out with his father. "My mom and I were getting ice cream at this place called Bobbie's Dairy Dip in Nashville," Swift said. "We pull up, and I'm eating ice cream, and my mom looks over and goes, 'Look at that little boy!' We literally walked up to him . . . and said, 'I know this is really weird, but I'm shooting a music video, and your son's really cute. Do you want to go to Maine?' And they all ended up doing it."

FUN FACTS The "Mine" video was filmed in July 2010 in Kennebunkport, Maine, at the Ram Island Farm in Cape Elizabeth and at Christ Church on Dane Street (for the wedding scene). "The first day we shot at this private estate," recalled director Roman White. "They had a private beach and everything, which made shooting a lot easier, because when you go out in public and somebody spots Taylor Swift, I mean, it doesn't take 15 minutes and there's a huge crowd." Taylor wanted the locals who helped her make her video to see their town onscreen first, so CMT and the Swift One came back to Maine for an advance screening. Among the 800 attendees was former President George H.W. Bush, who brought his grandchildren.

DID YOU NOTICE? The photos in the trees are of Taylor, Toby, and the kids in the videos; as Taylor described in her Vevo Certified commentary, "They're all really legit pictures in the trees." Add two more white dresses to the count, plus a wedding gown!

"BACK TO DECEMBER"

THE CONCEPT Isolation and cold play a big role in this video, where Taylor mourns her breakup alone in her apartment, while her former beau wanders the wintry landscape. The two never interact, save for a letter of apology that Taylor tucks into his jacket pocket, which he discovers at the end. Interestingly, the concept was in part inspired by *E.T.*: French director Yoann Lemoine (who's directed videos for Katy Perry, Lana Del Ray, and Drake) thought of the connection between Elliot and E.T., and emulated that in Taylor's character feeling the cold that her ex is experiencing outside. "Something I really liked about the song was the very emotional side of it, and how I could play with the winter theme of it," he explained. "Like how there is that parallel between the feelings she is having and the coldness of snow. I wanted to draw out the way that he is outside, but she is the one who is cold because they are connected. He's freezing, but she's feeling pain." As Taylor put it, "It's snowing *inside*. It's like there's nowhere I could go to escape from this figurative precipitation."

GUEST STARRING Model Guntars Asmanis has appeared in campaigns for Prada, Louis Vuitton, Missioni, and Miu Miu among others. Lemoine explained to MTV that he wanted to cast "a boy that was fragile and beautiful. I didn't want to go for a hunk or a perfect cheesy boy that would have killed the sincerity of the video . . . both Taylor and I loved Guntars."

FUN FACTS The "Back to December" video was shot in two locations, fittingly in December 2010. Guntars' scenes were shot in snowy MacArthur Park and in Binghamton, near Syracuse, New York. Taylor's scenes were shot in a house outside of Nashville. Taylor and her onscreen ex never crossed paths while filming the video.

Lemoine wanted to shoot the video in a naturalistic visual style, to fit the heartbreak of the lyrics. "I wanted people to feel like they would get to know her very intimately, and really trust in what she was saying," he explained. "I wanted her to perform a very natural way, to make her look very European. This was the main challenge to me. All of Taylor's world is very far away from my culture, but I saw something in her that could be very rough and heartbreaking, far from the princess glittery outfits and glam that she often goes for."

DID YOU NOTICE? There's a birdcage in the bedroom, just like in Taylor's Nashville apartment. To create the snowing-inside effect, the crew used two different kinds of fake snow: a dry, confetti-like snow and another that Taylor described as "really cold, really wet — it's like jelly snow and jelly snow is like . . . really-strange-consistency-apple-sauce snow," or more succinctly, "gucky." The goosebumps visible on Taylor were thanks to the very cold house and Taylor being "naturally a really cold person": "I'm, like, frail and always shivering. I'm like one of those little dogs that needs a sweater."

"THE STORY OF US"

THE CONCEPT The quiet tension of a college library explodes into a raucous paper-flying party and the standoff between Taylor and her love interest is at the center of it all. There's also a lot of action in the stacks, including a messy-haired Taylor going crazy. Though the video is replete with bookishness, this is one love story without a fairytale happy ending, as Taylor and her guy head in separate directions once the tension breaks.

GUEST STARRING After a two-video absence, Taylor's band is back, rocking out in the collegiate setting. Recognize the girl locking lips in the stacks? It's Taylor's longtime backup singer, Liz Huett.

FUN FACTS Taylor took director Noble Jones' idea to set the video in a library and made it Ivy League, an appropriate location for a girl now out of her teens. As for the preppy wardrobe, Taylor was stoked, telling MTV, "I've always wanted to do a video with that kind of style." They filmed at Vanderbilt University's Central Library and Alumni Hall in Nashville; Taylor loves walking through the campus when she's out grabbing coffee. A tornado hit during the shoot, causing filming to halt and, in Taylor's words, "we had to hide in a room where there were no windows, so that was a little bit crazy."

DID YOU NOTICE? In the opening shot of the video, when *The Story of Us* book is pulled from the shelf, it's alongside volumes about "Famous Women" — fitting for a Taylor Swift video.

"MEAN"

THE CONCEPT The empowerment and anti-bullying themes of "Mean" play out in a number of different storylines: Taylor and her band go from humble beginnings to the glitz of success; a boy picked on for being into fashion ends up a star designer; a girl working hard to save for school survives the teasing and gets her dream job; and middle school torment (something Taylor remembers well) is made more bearable for the girl eating lunch alone in the bathroom with a private Taylor Swift show. Explained director Declan Whitebloom, "We wanted to make something stunning while still getting the point across. They're stories that you've seen before in other videos, but we wanted to present it in a more visual and theatrical way." In a symbolic move, Taylor as a silent-screen damsel-in-distress realizes she can untie herself to escape from the train tracks and the mustache-twirling villain who is victimizing her.

GUEST STARRING Joey King, best known as Ramona to Selena Gomez's Beezus in *Ramona and Beezus*, plays the girl rejected by the popular crowd.

FUN FACTS The video was nominated for an MTV VMA social activism award. Part of its success may come down to the collaborative spirit between star and director. "After I wrote my treatment, her management called me to tell me she liked it, because it was so evocative of the one already in her mind," Whitebloom said. "We got on really well. It's rare when you connect with an artist that quickly, but we

"SPARKS FLY"

THE CONCEPT Like her "Fearless" tour video before it, this clip showcases Taylor live on her tour for *Speak Now*. Directed by Christian Lamb, the video uses both slow and fast motion footage to highlight the most epic moments of the show.

GUEST STARRING It's all about Taylor, her adoring fans, and her much-loved band.

FUN FACTS The amazing footage of Taylor and her band performing in a total downpour is at Gillette Stadium, in Foxborough, Massachusetts, in June 2011. After that show, Taylor tweeted, "Tonight I got to dance in the pouring rain with 52,000 people. I will NEVER forget it."

DID YOU NOTICE? If you take a close look at the lyrics written down Taylor's arm, you can piece together which tour stop she is on in that footage.

"OURS"

THE CONCEPT Taylor joins the working world in this video, for a day in the life at a boring job that's (thankfully) punctuated by moments of "subtle comedy." For Taylor's character, this day is different from the rest. She has something major to look forward to: the boyfriend we see her cavorting with in home movies returns from army service. Explained Taylor, "I just love the contrast of seeing someone light up when they're with someone they love, whereas they can be living in tones of gray when they're not."

GUEST STARRING It's Matt Saracen! Zach Gilford, best known for playing the soulful underdog QB1 on *Friday Night Lights*, is, as Taylor put it, "really endearing in all the roles

share a quirky, offbeat sense of humor." Shot in L.A.'s Orpheum Theatre over two days, the video's vintage look was inspired by the album art and Taylor's onstage style at the ACMs. Even though Taylor wanted to tell the story of "Mean" through other characters, that didn't mean she was less than totally into the production process. "She was keenly involved in writing the treatment, casting, and wardrobe. And she stayed for both the 15-hour shooting days, even when she wasn't in the scenes," said Whitebloom.

DID YOU NOTICE? The backdrop behind Taylor and her band when they've hit the big time lists both Hollywood and Nashville — the cities that signify success for Ms. Swift.

he plays." This was his first music video.

FUN FACTS Shot in a drab office building, on a Nashville city bus, at the Nashville International Airport, and at a house that was styled as the characters' "starter home," director Declan Whitebloom changed the filming style and lighting from one half of the video to the next to express the lift in spirits Taylor has as she escapes the office and goes to meet Zach. For the home movie segments, Taylor and Zach held the camera and shot most of the footage themselves to give it an unprofessional feel and to capture the right perspective. Unusually, there is no separate performance set-up (Taylor singing to camera, looking pretty); instead it's all in character, which was Taylor's idea. Each artistic and production choice was made to drive home Taylor's main concept: that happiness is fleeting, and you have to fight for those moments.

DID YOU NOTICE? The elevator stops on the 13th floor. Though it's mostly miserable at the office (darn photocopier, always out of toner!), there is a smiley face made of push-pins on the corkboard by the water cooler. Taylor's promotional relationship with Sony gets another hit here with some Sony Tablet S product placement.

"SAFE AND SOUND"

THE CONCEPT Fittingly for the first single off *The Hunger Games*' soundtrack album, Taylor wanders through a forest that looks straight out of Panem. For Taylor, it was essential that Suzanne Collins' story be honored: "Everyone who is a Hunger Games fan knows what it means when there's fire in the trees, and they know what it means for the house to be burnt, and they know what it means for the [mock-

ingjay] pin to be covered in rust and old. Everybody can take their own meaning away from it, but it all goes back to the symbolism of the book."

GUEST STARRING The Civil Wars are featured in a derelict house, not unlike the Everdeens' in the film.

FUN FACTS Directed by Philip Andelman and shot in a forest in Watertown, Tennessee, the simple video features Taylor in little makeup and a vintage nightgown. Though the concept and song are hauntingly understated, the impact was huge. The video received a global release across all of Viacom Music Group's channels around the world, reaching an estimated 600 million viewers.

DID YOU NOTICE? In part of the video, Taylor is on a real gravestone. "It's one of my favorite moments in the video," revealed Taylor. "There's this wide shot, where I'm just kind of crumpled up sitting on a gravestone, and it's actually the gravesite of a couple who lived and died in 1853. I'm sitting here thinking, 'What were their lives like?' It's really eerie, considering what the movie is about and how it deals with life and death. It just absolutely blew my mind."

"WE ARE NEVER EVER GETTING BACK TOGETHER"

THE CONCEPT With whimsy and playfulness, the video for the lead single off *Red* follows the relationship drama that Taylor is so totally over. Its biggest accomplishment is that it is filmed in a single continuous take — an incredible achievement that required a great deal of coordination and careful timing.

GUEST STARRING Taylor's band is back and, no

explanation required, wearing woodland creature costumes. The boyfriend she is never ever ever getting back together with is played by model/actor Noah Mills.

FUN FACTS Director Declan Whitebloom was at the helm again, with a crack team to make the one-continuous-shot concept a reality. To achieve it, they used five connected sets: the rooms of the apartment had a trick wall that backed away to a "split-screen" setup of Taylor on the phone and her boyfriend calling from the bar. Then there was the cardboard cut-out car with rear projection and the park where the seasons change, which then circles back to the first set. Off-camera, there were areas called "car washes" where Taylor was meant to do her costume changes, but with the timing so tight she never made it to them. The quick-change wardrobe team that works with Taylor on her tours was on hand to flip her outfits lickety split.

Cinematographer Paul Laufer explained that, despite its complexity, the one-take scene only took six hours to film: "Not too long because Taylor is so good. I don't think she made a single mistake, which is incredible when you see the costume changes and her performance. It's uncanny, because she was staying in the moment where her performance was right on and committed. And then a split second later, the camera would be off her and she would have to drop out of frame, change clothes, run around the back of the set, and appear in character in the next scene. And I'm talking split seconds — it is all done practically. What you see is real. There are absolutely no camera tricks."

The other star of the video was behind the camera, explained Laufer. "Gustavo Penna, operator of the camera stabilized rig, was fantastic. He nailed it time and time and time again. Obviously everything was on audible cues. What really helped was that he is actually a classically trained pianist, and therefore his timing and understanding of music and changes really played into that. He is also a ballroom dancer, which he says works incredibly well with his rig. He sees the camera as a dance partner. He was definitely in the zone the whole time."

DID YOU NOTICE? Gossip sites and fans alike were curious as to who the ditched boyfriend was and looked for clues in the video: was the scarf a reference to Jake Gyllenhaal? Is the watch she's wearing the one he gave her? Some of the details may be carefully planted clues, but Taylor was also embracing randomness, as she told the *New York Times*. "You know when you watch an indie video and you're like, 'Why are they underwater in upside-down chairs with a random projection of a butterfly interspersed? Why is this happening?' We were trying to think of ways that we could tip our hat to the randomness of some indie music videos. Why are there woodland creatures? Nobody knows. Why am I wearing floral-print pajamas? Nobody knows. Why am I randomly wearing glasses? Nobody knows."

"BEGIN AGAIN"

THE CONCEPT Alone in the City of Love, a particularly fashionable Taylor tours around the city on a bicycle before she finds a *très charmant garçon* at a café. Explained Taylor, "I think I've done that, where you wander around a city you're unfamiliar with and just kind of go out by yourself and go walking around."

GUEST STARRING Though there is the eye candy of the French model who plays Taylor's new crush (who taught her some French while filming), the true guest star of the video is stunning Paris. "That city was like a character in the video," said Taylor. "It's a beautiful, incredible place to be."

FUN FACTS The video was shot by Philip Andelman ("Safe and Sound") on September 30 and October 1, 2012, in various parts of Paris (she rides her *bicyclette* around Place de Furstenberg and Saint-Germain-des-Prés). Perhaps her most stylish video to date, Taylor models some high fashion, most notably a Maria Lucia Hohan lavender silk mousseline dress in the rooftop shot with the Eiffel Tower in the background.

DID YOU NOTICE? In a nod to her album title, Taylor sports red pants with a white sweater from Valentino's Red collection. And, yes, those are little cats on Taylor's flats as she cycles around the city.

"I KNEW YOU WERE TROUBLE"

THE CONCEPT Taylor's little-bit-country style goes a lot rock 'n' roll (thanks in part to that pink-highlighted wig) in a video that sees her falling for a bad boy. The reckless fun and cavorting takes a turn for slam-dancing, bar fights, skeezy motel rooms, and heartache, leaving Taylor alone in the morning-after detritus of a wild desert party. "I wanted to tell the story of a girl who falls into a world that's too fast for her, and suffers the consequences," explained Taylor.

GUEST STARRING Wooing Taylor with his tattoos and carefree attitude is Reeve Carney. A man of many talents, the actor is best known for his

stage work, playing Peter Parker/Spiderman on Broadway in *Spiderman: Turn Off the Dark*. He's musical himself, a guitar player and singer; check out "New to You" on the soundtrack for *The Twilight Saga: Breaking Dawn, Part 2*. Said Reeve of Taylor in the video, "It was a great acting piece for her . . . I thought she was fantastic. I kept telling her, 'Man, you're such a natural. You've got to do more of this.' And I don't know if she was listening to me or not, but I think she definitely has a natural ability." Taylor was just as impressed with Reeve, who did his own stunts in the video. "It's insane, like . . . how's he standing up and driving?"

FUN FACTS Never one to, you know, sleep, Taylor went to the video set in L.A. straight after the AMAs where she did a stunning performance of the song. She tweeted her thanks for the AMA win along with, "Long day but so worth it." Directed by Anthony Mandler, the video debuted on MTV on Taylor's 23rd birthday, and it was her 23rd video. Taylor wanted to make a starkly different video from her previous ones, and she succeeded. "To be frank, she came to me with the intention of doing something completely different," said Mandler to MTV News, "and that was the mantra from the beginning: 'I want to do something that is radically different, I want to play a character, I want to be somebody else, and I want to tell a really intense story that people can relate to' . . . and then the process was 'Okay, what's the story and how far can we actually *go*? What was she actually comfortable with? And what was maybe pushing *too* far?'"

DID YOU NOTICE? The narration that bookends the video was written by Taylor near the end of the filming. She and the director "riffed" on lines, and he was impressed with "just how well she understood this character."

"22"

THE CONCEPT Taylor brings the fun of the song's infectious lyrics to life in this video that sees Taylor and friends living like they're 22: goofing around in the kitchen, cavorting poolside and beachside, dancing, getting dolled up to hit the town.

GUEST STARRING Taylor didn't have to do much acting for the "22" video: her real-life friends — including Claire Kislinger, Ashley Avignone, and actress Jessica Szohr — joined her in front of the cameras for the gallivanting good times. After filming the video, Taylor took to Twitter to say, "Leaving L.A. now after the best day with my friends. Almost forgot it was a video shoot. Can't wait for you guys to see it."

FUN FACTS "I Knew You Were Trouble" director Anthony Mandler was back filming Taylor and friends in this clip, which was shot in Malibu, California, on February 11. Never one to let a 13 go by unacknowledged, Taylor debuted this video on *Good Morning America* on Red Tour kickoff date March 13, 2013.

DID YOU NOTICE? Fans theorized that Taylor's army-green hat was a "make fun of our exes moment": One Direction's Harry Styles is known for wearing that style hat. Taylor brought many true-to-life touches to the video: she dons cat ears (which she has on multiple occasions IRL) and the girls jump on a trampoline (and Taylor totally has one in her own backyard). Claire Kislinger gets the honor of lip-syncing the "Who's Taylor Swift, anyway?" line.

CHAPTER 14

BEYOND THE MUSIC

As if being a multi-platinum, award-winning recording artist who could sell out an international tour wasn't impressive enough, Taylor Swift has managed to tackle even more.

Though she had acted in community-theater shows as a kid, Taylor's first acting jobs in front of a camera were her music videos where she'd act out the storyline of her songs alongside professional actors. She also got used to being in front of cameras during interviews, especially in-depth ones like the GAC *Shortcuts* documentary about her, and in shows like MTV's *Once Upon a Prom*. In June 2008, MTV cameras followed Taylor and Abigail as they attended prom at Hillcrest High School in Alabama. Said Taylor, "My senior year I got to go to a prom . . . and took my best friend and we both had dates we never met before. But it was fun!" Taylor loves including her bestie in her adventures and Abigail is happy to join in: "It's a great opportunity for somebody my age to just follow her. I'm not so much following in her footsteps, but just getting to experience and witness what somebody goes through when they become a celebrity or they are in the limelight. Any opportunity she gives me like that, I definitely take it." Abigail, a three-time All-American and four-time "Swimmer of the Year" at Hendersonville High, went on to Kansas University's varsity swim team and its journalism program. Her distance from Hendersonville and the rigors of being a school-record-breaking varsity athlete combined with Taylor's crazy schedule means the

best friends have to work hard to see each other. But their friendship is so strong that they're inseparable even when physically apart.

Taylor paired another close personal relationship with time in front of the cameras when she made her big-screen debut in *Jonas Brothers: The 3D Concert Experience*, which was released in theaters in February 2009. She was pretty familiar with her role: she played herself and sang "Should've Said No" with the brothers Jonas. At the time, she was dating Joe Jonas, about whom "Forever & Always" was later written. The two had decided not to go public with their relationship though gossip columnists correctly pegged the pair as a couple. It was only after the infamous 27-second phone call during which Joe broke up with Taylor that she decided it was open season; she discussed the breakup on *Ellen*, and posted a comical video telling a Taylor Swift doll to stay away from a Joe Jonas doll.

Taylor didn't let a bad breakup keep her down when she had another milestone right around the corner. A natural onscreen, Taylor had said she was "definitely open to acting roles; it just depends on the story." She didn't have to wait long for the right role to be offered to her. A huge fan of *CSI* ("I like intense shows about intense things"), Taylor was over the moon when she was cast as murder victim Haley Jones in the episode "Turn, Turn, Turn," which aired on March 5, 2009. Her episode drew a season-high viewership of almost 21 million people.

She was back on the big screen in April, working with another one of her friends, Miley Cyrus, in *Hannah Montana: The Movie*. In a cameo appearance, Taylor played the unnamed girl singing in the barn; the song she sang was "Crazier," which appeared on the movie's soundtrack. Taylor is close pals with Miley (who also spends time near Nashville in Franklin) along with two other former "Disney girls," Demi Lovato and Selena

Gomez. Says Taylor, "It's really awesome to get to hang out with those girls and to call them friends." Sometimes she forgets the age difference between them: "I feel like Miley, Selena, and Demi are my age. It's crazy." The girls may not always get to see one other with their busy lifestyles but they are always there for each other. Before Miley's AMA performance in 2008, which happened to be on her sweet 16 birthday, Taylor and the girls arranged for a big birthday cake backstage to surprise her. For Demi's birthday, Taylor gave her mace, "because I don't want anything to happen to [her]. Demi loved it, and her dad loved it too." Taylor and Selena would talk on the phone every day, as do Taylor did with actress Emma Stone (*The Help*).

In the first week of November 2009, some of those phone calls must have been about Taylor's upcoming appearance as host and musical guest on the legendary sketch comedy show *Saturday Night Live*. Back in January, she had been the youngest country artist to be the musical guest, and that experience landed in Taylor's top three "pinch-yourself" moments. As host of the November 7th episode, she appeared in numerous skits and performed two songs; some of her more memorable moments included playing Bella in a *Twilight* parody (where the dreamy vampire was replaced by a less-than-dreamy Frankenstein monster) and her "Monologue Song (La La La)," where she mocked her music, her love of all things sparkly, and the Kanye West incident at the 2009 MTV VMAs.

The other hot topic in her monologue was her relationship with *Twilight* actor Taylor Lautner. The two met while filming the star-studded romantic comedy *Valentine's Day*. That film, directed by Garry Marshall, was Taylor's official big-screen acting debut and her plot line involved a romance with the other Taylor. It was confusing for the crew to have two Taylors on set, so girl Taylor suggested that instead she be called "Swifty" (her band's nickname for her). Once the cameras stopped rolling, the two Taylors continued to spend time together. They were spotted at a hockey game and out for dinner, but neither officially confirmed their relationship. Before the media had settled on a cutesy name for them (Taylor Squared?), the romance had ended. Those curious for more gossip had to wait for Taylor's heartfelt apology song, "Back to December," to find out how this love story had ended. Always a class act, Taylor Swift showed her support for Taylor Lautner by giving him a standing ovation when he won a 2010 People's Choice Award. In Japan on Valentine's Day 2010, Swifty missed the U.S. premiere of *Valentine's Day* but her song on its soundtrack, "Today Was a Fairytale," didn't miss the mark at all. It debuted on the Billboard Hot 100 at number two.

With television and film credits now on her list of accomplishments, Taylor got into the gaming universe when the creators of *Guitar Hero* approached her to be a part of their spin-off project, *Band Hero*, which was released in November 2009. Performing "Love Story," "You Belong with Me," and "Picture to Burn," a digital version of Taylor, modeled on real-life Taylor, appears onstage with "magical sparkles" swirling around her. Taylor advises people to do some neck exercises before play-

Taylors Swift and Lautner film a scene in *Valentine's Day*.

ing her avatar since there's a lot of hair swinging going on in her performance. Joked Taylor, "Hair as well as guitar are the instruments that I use."

There's no end to the opportunities being offered to the superstar. Taylor picked up a gig as an NHL spokesperson, appearing in commercials for the Nashville Predators and debuting the team's new jersey design in con-

cert in 2009. Like everything else in her career, Taylor only agreed to do it because it's something she actually loves. When she has time off, she often heads to a Predators game.

While that endorsement deal was close to home, Taylor's highest-profile gig was less cross-checks and offsides and more smizing and hair blowing in the wind. CoverGirl announced that Taylor would be the

Taylor and her dear friend Selena Gomez at the Hope for Haiti Now telethon on January 22, 2010. Said Taylor of Selena: "It is very easy for girls to get caught up in Hollywood and the spotlight, and they become different. And I feel like the people that I've been lucky to meet and be friends with are still really real people."

spokesperson for its new NatureLuxe makeup line, debuting in January 2011. A perfect fit for the brand, and a natural in front of the camera, Taylor wasn't shy to poke a little light-hearted fun at her new gig when fellow CoverGirl and friend Ellen invited her to show off her modeling skills on an episode of *Ellen*. Though Taylor's signature look —

"It was really neat. Total blonde power. After the game, we pulled into a gas station and Carrie saw this guy talking to Taylor. We were like, This isn't right! I said, 'Get away from her, you old man. If you're still around when we finish filling up with gas, we'll make a hood ornament out of you!'"
— Kellie Pickler on a girls' night out at a hockey game with Taylor and Carrie Underwood.

cat eyeliner in black and red-red lips — is simple and iconic, she has been known to experiment from time to time. When shooting her cover story for *Vogue*'s February 2012 issue, Taylor was cool with the stylist chopping her hair to give her a blunt bang, right there on set. "It turned out to be one of my favorite changes I've ever made to my hair,"

said Taylor. "Moral of the story: always trust *Vogue*."

Back on more familiar ground in the studio, Taylor's eclectic music taste has led her to a number of collaborations over the years — some more predictable than others. One of her first was with pal and touring buddy Kellie Pickler ("Best Days of Your Life"), but soon after that she was reaching out to other songwriters publicly. After expressing interest in working with John Mayer, the two hooked up on the track "Half of My Heart," which was released in November 2009. Mayer thought of the song as a "sort of Tom Petty, Fleetwood Mac, Stevie Nicks thing," and said, "'Well, if this is going to be my love letter to that style of music, who's going to be the Stevie Nicks in this equation?' And I thought, 'This Taylor Swift girl is going to be around for a long time.'" Famously, this duet lead to romance and eventually inspired some of Taylor's most passionate songs of heartbreak. Thankfully, not all of her musical matchups have been quite so traumatic for Taylor: she sang on the Boys Like Girls' track "Two Is Better Than One" (2009) and on B.o.B.'s thoughtful "Both of Us" (2012).

When legendary producer T. Bone Burnett was looking for artists to contribute to the soundtrack for *The Hunger Games*, Taylor was keen to join the list of notable artists like Arcade Fire and Neko Case. For the album's lead single, released December 23, 2011, Taylor wrote and recorded with The Civil Wars on "Safe and Sound." John Paul White, of the Nashville-based band, told CMT.com, "I think it's very brave of her to step slightly away from what she normally does. There's

probably more of a melancholic vibe than she typically pulls off. It makes perfect sense in the trajectory of what she's doing. She's growing and maturing and reaching out. I think the sky's the limit for the types of things that she can do in the future. We were more than happy to maybe darken the world up for her." The song nabbed two Grammy nominations, Best Country Duo/Group Performance and Best Song Written for Visual Media (which they won), and Taylor got a special birthday surprise when the song also got a Golden Globe nom for Best Original Song — Motion Picture, announced on December 13. Taylor wrote a second song for the soundtrack album, "Eyes Open," about "Katniss's relationship with the Capitol."

Always looking for a new challenge, Taylor got to be a part of an animated feature film when she was cast as the voice of Aubrey in *The Lorax*. Explained Taylor, "The reason I said yes right away was just because as a kid, [Dr. Seuss] was my first exposure to poetry. That was the first time I'd ever realized that if you put words in a certain combination, and you put the right rhymes at the end of the right phrases, you can make words absolutely bounce off a page." Though Taylor was voicing the love interest of Zac Efron's character, the two weren't huddled in a recording studio together to make the movie. "It turns out you're in a studio all by yourself, talking to yourself," said Taylor, "and creating a character based on what her voice sounds like." After seeing the movie, which premiered on March 2, 2012, she was so proud to have been a part of it, describing the family friendly flick as "such a fun movie, and then [the audience is] going to walk out of the theaters thinking about their lives and how to better preserve the environment."

Though rumors swirled in the summer of 2012 that Taylor had been cast to play Joni Mitchell in the film adaptation of Sheila Weller's book *Girls Like Us* and *Variety* reported it as confirmed, Taylor was shy to cement it as fact until the project was definitely underway. As she told *Time* about her acting aspirations, "I would love to sign on to do a movie if it was the right role and if it was the right script, because I would be taking time away from music to tell a big grand story, and spend all of my time and pouring all of my emotions into being someone else. So for me to do that, it would have to be a story worth telling." With Taylor's huge admiration for Joni Mitchell, this just may be the right role.

No matter how much Taylor's day-to-day life changes to become more like an international superstar's — complete with multiple homes, world tours, her face on billboards worldwide, and millions of fans — she is focused on staying grounded. None of her friendships are "industry-centric," even those with other young celebs. With Selena Gomez, she talks about everything a typical 20-something would. "I would say Selena is my most fun, spontaneous, energetic friend," said Taylor. "If she says, 'Hey let's do this!,' I'm like, 'OK!' Because I know it's going to be hilarious and she's always up for an adventure, but at the same time you can sit down and say I'm going through something crazy and I need someone to talk to, and she'll listen to you." The same goes for romance: she wants it to be as "normal" as possible. Taylor doesn't want to hide away for privacy's sake; though sneaking out the back exit of a restaurant after a dinner date may prevent the paparazzi from snapping pics of Taylor and her latest flame, it makes her "feel like a fugitive." As she explained to British chat show host Alan Carr, "I'd just rather live my life. I feel like if you can be in a relationship and have it seem normal — that would be good." In terms of new guys who enter her life, she figures it is so well known now that she writes songs about her relationships, she feels "like they're signing a release form." Though Taylor is so often an open book, she steadfastly refuses to kiss and tell in interviews; as she's fond of saying, "I just think that my personal stories sound better in a song than in an interview in quotes."

Though Taylor has had all of her dreams come true thanks to her tireless efforts, she's not without worries or anxiety. As she told Katie Couric before the release of *Red*, "My life has become like a constant balancing act between hope and fear, faith and worrying, being nervous about this album that I've worked really hard on and being proud of this album that I've worked really hard on." At the helm of an international pop phenomenon, Taylor has a lot of work to take care of that has nothing to do with the art of songwriting. But Taylor recognizes how crucial it is to her success and, more importantly, to her happiness. "The business aspect is one of the most important things about having a music career, because every choice you make in a management meeting affects your life a year and a half from now. I know exactly where I'm going to be next year at this time. That's because I'm sitting there in those management

meetings every single week and scheduling everything and approving things, or not approving things, based on what I feel is right for my career at this point."

Despite her hectic schedule and high profile, in many ways Taylor is still a regular young woman. She loves watching *Girls* and crime shows like *Law and Order: SVU*, and prefers hiking over going to the gym — with her iPod on, she can exercise without feeling like she's exercising; "forest, butterflies, music!" But she knows that there's a bigger penalty for her if she were to make the same missteps as others outside of the spotlight. She very deliberately didn't drink until she was legally allowed to do so, and is careful to drink identifiable beverages when she's out and could be photographed by the paparazzi. "I like to have fun and I like to be happy and have a level of spontaneity in my life, and go off on a whim here," said Taylor. "That's the part of my brain that's an artist, and then there's the part of my brain that also understands that there's a harsh reality to every single one of my actions. So those two are fighting all the time too."

On the Swedish talk show *Skaylan*, Taylor confessed, "My life is a constant balance of understanding that I can't control everything, and I can't control what people are going to think about me, and I can't control what people are going to write about me, but I can control my actions and how I live my life. I overthink things a lot. I always want to make the right choice, not for the sake of how it's perceived, but because I do understand that I'm living a life, and I'm going to have to look back on that life 20 years from now, if I'm lucky, and be proud of the choices that I made. 'Cause it is intense being 22 and having, like, a magnifying glass on you."

The philosophical mood strikes Taylor often and she's not afraid to share the guiding principles she follows: "I think a lot about life. I think a lot about future regrets, and trying to avoid them. When you talk to people who are in their 70s and 80s and they talk about regrets they had in their life, it was not living in the moment, trying to grow up too fast, missing out on things 'cause they didn't look around and feel things, and not spending enough time with their friends and family. Those are things that I always really try to focus on. You know, trying to be a good human being. . . . That's more important than a career, or being a 'brand' — you're living a life."

Judging by the opinion of the person who arguably matters most to Taylor, her mom Andrea, there's no doubt she's living a life full of the right choices for her and remarkable achievements: "There are times when I look at this young woman and everything she's accomplished and where she is and yet I still see that little girl in the car seat with those big blue eyes in my rearview mirror, and I say that's my baby. And I'm real proud."

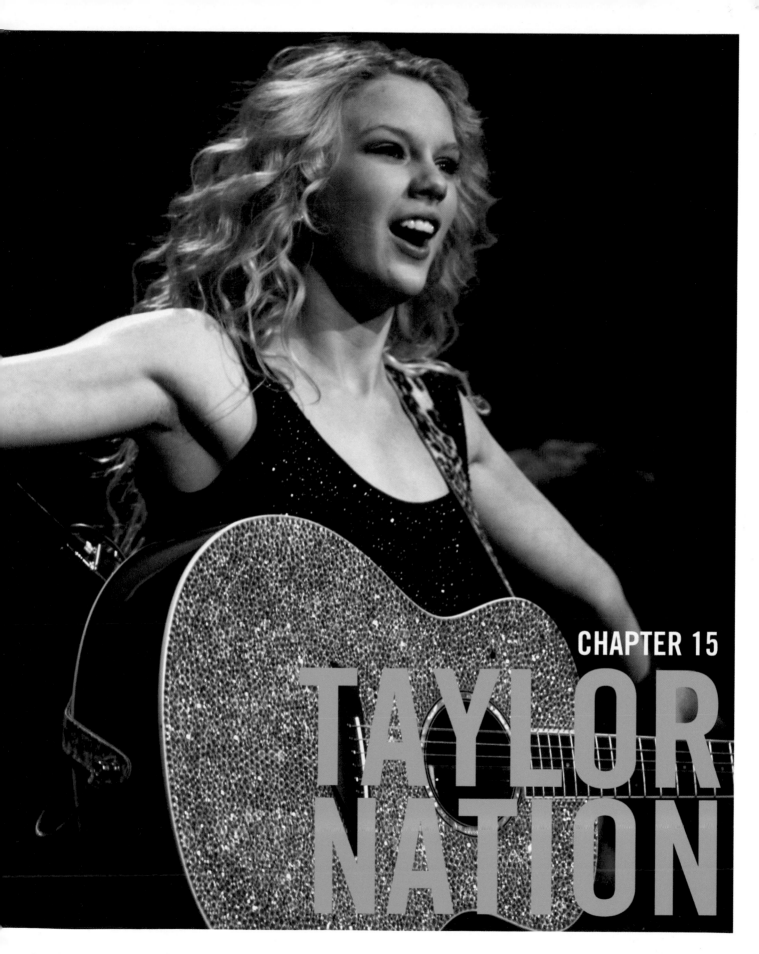

CHAPTER 15

TAYLOR NATION

Taylor Swift remembers what it was like to be a fan who idolized country singers. She once waited in line for hours to get LeAnn Rimes' autograph and she owned a life-size Brad Paisley stand-up poster. She admitted that even now that she has reached celebrity status, "I get starstruck all the time. I ask for autographs at award shows like a superfan." That's

There are lots of celebrities who take the time to stop for an autograph or a quick hello, but there are very few people willing to put on an impromptu show. Luckily for her fans, Taylor is one of them.

One day at the Nashville airport while Taylor and her band were waiting for a flight, some fans approached the local celebrity and asked her to play a song. Taylor told *Allure*, "They saw my guitar sitting there. So I got my band members to bust out their guitars too, and we just played a concert at the terminal. It's so much fun doing stuff like that."

On another occasion, Taylor and her band stopped into a Fresno, California, ice cream shop for a sweet treat and discovered that the woman working at the register was a huge T-Swift fan. That fan got a treat of her own when the band brought in their instruments and put on a private show right there in the shop! In an interview with the local paper, Taylor explained, "When people tell me they like my music, they have no idea how good that makes me feel. I take every opportunity I can to make it up to them."

part of the reason she treats her fans well, but the other reason is the obvious one — she wouldn't be where she is today without them. They buy her concert tickets and albums, request her songs on the radio, and help her win fan-voted awards like American Music Awards, Teen Choice Awards, and CMT Music Awards.

For some celebrities, fans are just faceless screaming masses, and they treat them that way. But Taylor gives her fans all the respect they deserve as people, and tries to make each fan encounter special. "If I sign an autograph for someone, I don't put them in the category of 'fan' and keep them at arm's length," she told *Self.* "If we strike up a conversation and we like the same things and we have the same sense of humor, then they're my friend. It doesn't matter how I met them."

— LOVE LOVE LOVE T —

One of the earliest ways Taylor interacted with her fans was through MySpace. Many musicians made MySpace pages with the express purpose of promoting their work; Taylor made hers just because "all my friends had MySpaces, and that's how they talked to each other. So I wanted to be cool too, and I wanted to make a MySpace." As an aspiring musician it was only natural for her to post music, and soon enough her talent spread like wildfire. MySpace was one of the first and easiest ways for new listeners to hear her music. She told CMT, "That was not a clever scheme. That was an accident . . . I didn't expect for MySpace to be a thing that propelled my career or was this huge army that it's become."

What Taylor valued most about MySpace is the chance to directly communicate with her fans who tell her how her music affects them. Andrea Swift told GAC, "They come on and tell their life story and why the song has meant so much to them and that's where it becomes a real personal thing. They're sharing. They're sharing their lives with Taylor." The reason fans feel comfortable sharing their lives with Taylor is that she's also sharing her life with them.

As she started recording her first album, Taylor also began posting blogs about her experience. Her posts make up a candid, funny, and inspiring story that allows fans to share those moments. Taylor may write about an awards ceremony or her snoring cat, but the blend of insight into the music business and average-girl details make Taylor's journey all the more compelling and real. Even if she has a swanky tour bus and more money than most people will see in their lifetime, she still acts like the girl-next-door. She told *Glamour*, "I've never felt like I needed to tone down being seen as a regular person."

Taylor gave her fans even more insight into her world when she started posting videos on MySpace as well. The videos are a kind of all-access pass that invites fans right into Taylor's home or car or backstage at a show. It's exhilarating to be able to share in the joy of moments like Taylor's reaction to earning four CMA Award nominations. While so many other celebrities only present a carefully polished public persona, Taylor shows her true face — even if it's not wearing any makeup. The videos are compilations Taylor edits herself (and often she's the camera

operator too) and her do-it-yourself spirit lets fans get to know her even more through the goofy footage she chooses or the songs she plays in the background.

As much as Taylor gave on MySpace, she got back in the wonderful comments from fans. She revealed, "Going on MySpace immediately makes my day better. I may be thinking, 'My hair doesn't look right,' 'I don't like this outfit,' or 'I need to do this or that,' but when I log in, they're like, 'Your music has changed my life,' 'Your music got me through this breakup,' 'Your song means so much to me.' When people are constantly being loving to you, it's the nicest thing. It's just so cool. It's a constant stream of love."

Whenever she has the time, Taylor tries to reply and have a conversation with her fans. "I spend a lot of time [responding] to fan emails. It's really, really important to me to make sure people know that I love them, I appreciate them, and I'm nothing without them. I'll never forget about them," said the star. "I'll always be on MySpace as much as I possibly can, trying to get back to them. Sometimes I get so addicted to it that I can't stop commenting people back. There's always one more that's so sweet. I've stayed up all night doing it."

With over 2.9 million friends, over 775,000 comments, and over 285 million song plays, Taylor Swift is a MySpace success story. So much so that when the site launched MySpace Music, Taylor joined MySpace CEO Chris DeWolfe for the celebration on *Today*. But the real reason Taylor's been so successful goes beyond any website. At the end of her very personal MySpace profile introduction, Taylor took the time to show her connection to the people who have helped her make her dreams come true: "I'm a fan of fans. You are absolutely wonderful to me. I've got your back, just like you've had mine. To anyone who has gone out and bought my CD, or come to a show, or even turned my song up when it came on the radio, all I can say is thank you."

SUPERSTAR

Taylor remembers the first time she was recognized. It was July 27, 2006; "Tim McGraw" was her only song on the radio; and she was in the Boise, Idaho, airport when a woman approached her and said, "Taylor, I just love your song and want to wish you great things in your career." The young songstress thought the lady had been sent over by her mom or her label rep, but she knew Taylor from the radio and her just-released video. Taylor blogged, "This was the first time someone had actually KNOWN who I was and MY NAME. Wow. I just walked over and hugged her, and said . . . 'You're the first person who's ever done that, thank you.' It was an amazing moment to remember, and I always will."

Before long, anonymity would be a thing of the past as the golden-haired beauty could be spotted on TV and in magazines. Whether she's shopping or eating in a restaurant, people gravitate toward her, and Taylor always takes time out for her fans. This could get frustrating, but unlike some celebrities who constantly gripe about the high price of fame, Taylor acknowledges that she knew what she was getting into when she started her career. She told *Marie Claire*, "When you spend so much time daydreaming about

things like [being recognized], when that actually happens you don't ever complain about it. When I go to a restaurant, yeah I know that a line is probably going to form in front of the table, but didn't I always wish for that? Yeah, I did. So it's like, I never want to be the girl who wanted something so bad her whole life and then gets it and complains about it. I'm not going to be that girl."

Taylor also gets that her celebrity status is something *she* signed up for, not her friends. "I'll find out that a group of my friends went out to dinner," said Taylor, "but they wanted it to be a low-key night and not worry about people coming up to the table every other second and asking for autographs, so they didn't invite me. I can understand that."

Luckily since she lives in Nashville, Taylor is not plagued by the paparazzi as much as some of her friends in L.A. are. But when Taylor ends up in the City of Angels, she handles the intrusive photographers like a pro. She usually just ignores them, though she can't help noticing some of life's funny coincidences. One day she tweeted, "There's nothing quite like singing along in the car to @ladygaga 'paparazzi' while actually being chased by paparazzi."

Maybe part of the reason Taylor isn't too bothered by the paparazzi is that she never gives them any scandalous photos to sell. Unlike some infamous stars who lose themselves on the rollercoaster ride to the top, Taylor isn't caught up in the party scene. And it's not because she's forced to behave by her parents or management — she makes responsible decisions on her own. "It's not like I've been beaten down by some corporation that's

Says Taylor of the legions of devoted Swifties: "It's strange to feel so understood by such a large group of people, but I love it."

forcing me to always behave myself — I just naturally do," Taylor explained. "Sometimes people are fascinated by the fact that I don't care about partying, almost to the point where they think it's weird. I think when we get to the point where it's strange for you to not be stumbling around high on something at 19, it's a warped world." With a star that's rising higher every day, Taylor's not about to let herself get distracted. "My career is the only thing I think about. It's stronger than any alcohol, stronger than any drug, stronger than anything else you could try — so why should I do those things, you know?" Instead, Taylor's found a more constructive way to rebel, and she insists, "For me, rebelling is done with words."

Beyond what's best for her career, Taylor also thinks about what's best for her fans. With millions of young people looking up to her, she wants to set the best example possible. She explains, "Every time I'm faced with a decision or a choice, I think about the six-year-old girl in the front row of my concert, and what she'd think about it. Then I think about her mom, and what she'd think. I never lose sight of what's really important. To me, it's those girls."

She's also careful about how she chooses to present herself. She's arrived at photo shoots and requested new wardrobe options that would provide her with a bit more coverage. "I've gotten there and they had a wardrobe rack and the only things hanging on the wardrobe racks were bras and bustiers," she told the *Tennessean*. "I'm like, 'Cool. Where are the clothes?' 'Those are the clothes.' 'No, no, no. Let's get clothes. I wear clothes.'"

As careful and deliberate as Taylor's choices have always been, she has had the challenge of growing up in the public eye — but she was never alone. An army of Swifties come to her defense when gossip columnists, critics, or haters attack with their "words like knives and swords," and Taylor adores her fans right back. For every album that goes platinum or fan-voted award that she wins, Taylor knows that it is an accomplishment she shares. Of the huge moments in her career, she said, "These are things that have happened to me; these are not things that I have done on my own. You can't have a successful music career without millions of fans doing that for you."

Her ability to connect with the fans who love her music, who attend her shows, and who sing her lyrics at the top of their lungs is something the superstar cherishes, and refuses to let go of. "I've always had a huge goal of never becoming one of those guarded, semi-paranoid, privacy-obsessed celebrity people," said the thoughtful songstress. "I don't feel comfortable around people who always think someone's trying to get something from them. I like having friends, and I like having a lot of friends. You end up with a very small group of people that can be around you if you're very guarded. So, for me, I like to hug my fans and talk to them about their breakups and problems just like I did when I was 16.

"A lot has changed since then, but a lot hasn't as well. I don't want to be one of those people who doesn't trust anyone. How are people supposed to trust you if you don't trust anyone?"

CHAPTER 16

EVERY DAY IS A FAIRYTALE

THE TAYLOR SWIFT NEWS DIARY

EARLY 2004

★ After years of festivals, karaoke bars, and dreaming of success, Taylor is signed to a development deal with RCA. She has her foot in the door of a record company, but the deal offers no guarantee that she'll emerge with an album.

FALL 2004

★ Taylor is featured in the Abercrombie & Fitch "rising stars" national advertising campaign.

SPRING 2005

★ Taylor lands a job at Sony/ATV Publishing, which makes her the youngest staff songwriter they had ever hired.

AUGUST 2005

★ Like many people her age, Taylor takes her place on MySpace, which becomes the earliest way to hear her music, and later one of her best ways of staying connected to fans all over the world.

SEPTEMBER 2005

★ Taylor is one of the first performers signed by Scott Borchetta to his new label, Big Machine Records.

JUNE 2006

★ Taylor's first single, "Tim McGraw," hits the airwaves on the 19th, debuting at number 60 on the Hot Country Songs chart.

★ Taylor attends her first award show, the Academy of Country Music Awards in Las Vegas.

AUGUST 2006

★ Taylor makes her small-screen acting debut with her first music video, "Tim McGraw."

OCTOBER 2006

★ On October 24, 2006, Taylor releases her self-titled debut. She celebrates its launch on *Good Morning America*, which had declared her a breakout artist back in 2004. The singer is thrilled, telling GAC, "This is my chance to bring my music out of my bedroom where I'm writing it."

★ The performer joins her first major tour, opening nine shows for Rascal Flatts.

JANUARY 2007

★ *Taylor Swift* earns its gold certification (marking 500,000 albums sold).

★ The songstress hits the road with country legend George Strait.

APRIL 2007

★ Taylor attends the CMT Music Awards, where she takes home her first piece of mantel bling — "The Buckle" for Breakthrough Video of the Year for "Tim McGraw."

★ Taylor brings the Buckle on the road with her on Brad Paisley's Bonfires & Amplifiers Tour, where she bonds with future bestie Kellie Pickler.

MAY 2007

★ At the May 15th Academy of Country Music Awards, Taylor gives a performance to remember, playing her hit "Tim McGraw" for its namesake, and afterward goes up to shake the country legend's hand. She's nominated for Top Female Vocalist, but doesn't win.

JUNE 2007

★ Taylor plays the CMA Country Music Festival, where she discovers her debut album has gone platinum, just eight months after its release! Remembering

Taylor donated the pink pickup truck her record label gave her for her 18th birthday to the Victory Junction Gang, a camp for sick kids.

how far she'd come in such a short time, the performer wrote, "I went the first year as a volunteer (when I was 14) and helped out with getting artists to their radio interviews. Then last year, I was there signing autographs (nobody knew who I was, it was funny) and telling anyone who would listen that I had a single coming out called 'Tim McGraw' and would they please request it at radio . . . haha. Then one year later, there I was, receiving a platinum plaque for a million copies of my album sold . . . It's been a good year. :-)"

★ While the Brad Paisley Tour is on a break, Taylor joins up for a few shows with Kenny Chesney.

JULY 2007

★ The rising star opens for two of her country music heroes, power couple Tim McGraw and Faith Hill, on their Soul2Soul II tour.

★ *Taylor Swift* hits number one on the Billboard Country Albums chart.

SEPTEMBER 2007

★ While Taylor's all about being personal on her MySpace, she's smart about where to draw the line online, and this month she teams up with Tennessee Governor Phil Bredesen and the Tennessee Association of Chiefs of Police in a public education campaign to help prevent internet crimes against children.

OCTOBER 2007

★ On the 16th, just short of a year
after her first album, Taylor releases
a Christmas EP, *Sounds of the Season:
The Taylor Swift Holiday Collection.*

NOVEMBER 2007

★ Even with her recent Christmas release,
fans want more Taylor, and so on the
6th, the in-demand singer-songwriter
releases a deluxe edition of *Taylor Swift*
with four bonus tracks and fun extras

like her Grand Ole Opry debut.

★ Though her songs are climbing the charts and her records flying off the shelves, Taylor feels she has actually made it in country music when she is given the Horizon Award from the Country Music Association. It's a moment she still sings about: "It was the night things changed."

DECEMBER 2007

★ Taylor celebrates her 18th birthday on the 13th and gets the best gift ever: her

first number one after fans made "Our Song" their own.

★ Taylor rang in a new year full of possibilities on *Dick Clark's New Year's Rockin' Eve*. She had cause for celebration: her debut album was certified double platinum earlier that month.

FEBRUARY 2008

★ Taylor walks the most prestigious of music's red carpets, attending her first Grammy ceremony. Nominated for Best New Artist, she loses to Amy Winehouse.

Taylor and her dad, Scott. Scott loves teasing his daughter. At one award show, Taylor was wearing a gown "made of these giant gold rocks sewn together. Every once in a while, a big chunk would fall off. My dad trailed after me laughing and picking up each piece, going, 'eBay.'"

★ Though MTV's *TRL* didn't invite a lot of country artists to come through the studio, Taylor gets the chance for an intimate acoustic performance on February 27.

APRIL 2008

★ At the Miley and Billy Ray Cyrus–hosted CMT Music Awards, Taylor lights up the stage with a performance of "Picture to Burn" and takes home two awards for "Our Song" (Female Video of the Year and Video of the Year). Taylor recalled the moment she won Female Video, writing, "I will never forget the look on my mom's face when they called out my name as the winner of that award. . . . For the first time in my life, I was speechless. I had NO clue winning that was a possibility. I remember just looking out into the crowd and thinking 'How am I this lucky . . . How do I get to live this life . . . ?'"

★ At the untelevised Young Hollywood Awards, Taylor is dubbed Superstar of Tomorrow and awarded a pair of diamond earrings to add a little something to her natural sparkle.

★ *Taylor Swift* goes triple platinum. Taylor marks the occasion with an announcement on April 29 on *Good Morning America* — the same show she appeared on the day of the album's release less than two years earlier.

MAY 2008

★ The theatrical performer makes a splash with her tempestuous performance of "Should've Said No" at the 2008 ACM Awards, and takes home more hardware for Top New Female Vocalist. (She was also nominated for Album of the Year and Top Female Vocalist.)

★ Taylor solidifies her status as teen idol

Taylor was inspired by Britney Spears' early award-show performances where she would "always do something a little unexpected." Taylor, seen here with the pop idol at the MTV Video Music Awards, used to have a Britney poster on her wall at home.

by gracing the cover of *Seventeen*.

★ The star announces a partnership with L.e.i. jeans. The company is a good fit for Taylor who noted, "I love the jeans, and I love what L.e.i. stands for: Life. Energy. Intelligence."

JUNE 2008

★ Taylor returns to *TRL* for a week of

co-hosting, starting June 16.

★ Though Taylor missed a lot of the senior year experience, MTV ensures she doesn't miss her senior prom by inviting her to star in an episode of *Once Upon a Prom*, which aired June 21.

JULY 2008

★ To demonstrate her appreciation for all

of her team's hard work, Taylor takes her band, crew, and their families to Kona, Hawaii, for a vacation. Taylor blogged, "They've all worked so hard for the past two years without a real break . . . So I took everybody to Hawaii. It's been the most AMAZING week and we all needed it."

★ Taylor releases her limited edition EP *Beautiful Eyes*, which sells 45,000 copies in its first week, taking the number one position on the Billboard Country Chart, with *Taylor Swift* holding the number two spot.

★ Just a month behind her former classmates, Taylor receives her high-school diploma, graduating from the private Christian school Aaron Academy, which offers a homeschooling program. "Education has always been at the forefront of my priorities, so I'm really glad to have my diploma," Taylor told the Associated Press.

AUGUST 2008

★ With the *Fearless* release approaching, Taylor gets some news to help calm the pre-release jitters — *Taylor Swift* has earned its fourth platinum certification.

★ Remember when those record execs told Taylor there were no young country fans? Taylor proves them wrong with a Teen Choice Award for Choice Breakout Artist.

★ After Cedar Rapids, Iowa, suffered devastating flooding, Taylor announces during a performance that she will donate $100,000 to the Red Cross to help with the flood relief effort. She told *People*, "They've stood by me, they gave me a sold-out show. You've got to pay it forward in life — that's all I did in Cedar Rapids."

SEPTEMBER 2008

★ Taylor jumps across the pond for performances in London (or "Fundon" as Taylor calls it) on the 3rd.

★ Though the song goes "This ain't a fairytale," on September 26, it is the stuff of fairytales when Taylor hears "White Horse" played on one of her favorite TV shows, *Grey's Anatomy*.

★ Taylor is back on the red carpet as MTV's fashion correspondent for the VMAs. The singer is up for Best New Artist, but loses to German rock sensation Tokio Hotel.

OCTOBER 2008

★ Taylor sings the national anthem at game three of the World Series between the Philadelphia Phillies and the Tampa Bay Rays. Aside from years of anthem-singing experience, Taylor got the invite because she used to sing for the minor league Reading Phillies. It is a special moment for Taylor, and for some of the players too, who'd heard a much younger Taylor sing the anthem in their minor league days, and now they'd all made it to the big leagues!

NOVEMBER 2008

★ On November 8, CMT airs its *Crossroads* special, pairing Taylor with

Taylor with Joe Elliott of Def Leppard. She and her band love Def Leppard, so performing with them was a dream come true: "We were just looking at each other like, 'This is not happening, you've got to be kidding me.'"

Def Leppard, and proving Taylor's theory that good music breaks through the borders of genre.

★ After a two-year wait for Taylor's sophomore album, *Fearless* drops on November 11. In its first week, the album sells over 10 times the number of copies of Taylor's debut, hitting number one on the Billboard 200. There was no sophomore slump for this unstoppable star.

★ With a new line of dolls from Jakks Pacific, Taylor proves that even in plastic, she's fantastic! The dolls sport Taylor staples like sundresses and sparkly dresses, and even come equipped with her trademark sparkly guitar for composing heartbreak ballads about other dolls. Taylor notes, "I can't wait to see little girls play with my doll and rock out with my crystal guitar."

★ Taylor takes home three BMI Awards for her songwriting, and "Teardrops on My Guitar" is hailed as Country Song of the Year. When Taylor takes the stage to accept her award she gets two thumbs up from Hank Williams Jr. and a text message from Kenny Chesney saying, "Congrats, I love you."

★ Our golden girl gets glammed up for the CMAs, where she reenacts the "Love Story" video (complete with Justin Gaston), and is nominated for Female Vocalist of the Year. In the first three years of her career, this is the only CMA Award nomination she doesn't turn into a win.

★ The award-filled month continues when Taylor wins her first American Music Award for Favorite Female Country Artist. The young songstress is overcome with gratitude to her fans for voting for her. She wrote, "I can't tell you how thankful/amazed/excited/ecstatic/over-joyed/blown away I am that you won me my FIRST American Music Award! I've said it before, and I'll say it again now. . . . There's nothing like a fan-voted award."

★ Rumors fly that Taylor is pregnant. She responds on her MySpace blog calling it "the most IMPOSSIBLE thing on the plan-et. Take my word for it. Impossible," and tells *Access Hollywood*, "I didn't do anything to provoke that. Like I'm sitting there thinking, like what? Did I wear the wrong shirt?"

★ During her November 11 appearance on *Ellen*, Taylor drops a gossip bomb of her own when she admits that Joe Jonas broke up with her in a 27-second phone call.

DECEMBER 2008

★ Kellie Pickler releases "Best Days of Your Life," a single co-written by Taylor, which ends up staying on the charts for over 40 weeks.

★ On the 23rd, Taylor releases a live album, *iTunes Live from Soho*, that features the songstress performing eight tracks, including a cover of Rihanna's "Umbrella."

★ Taylor celebrates a year of unimaginable success with another performance in Times Square for *Dick Clark's New Year's*

Taylor paints a 13 on her hand before every show; it's her lucky number. "I was born on the 13th. I turned 13 on Friday the 13th. My first album went gold in 13 weeks. My first number-one song had a 13-second intro. Every time I've won an award I've been seated in either the 13th seat, the 13th row, the 13th section or row M, which is the 13th letter. Basically whenever a 13 comes up in my life, it's a good thing."

Rockin' Eve. The golden girl of 2008 sings a medley of "Should've Said No," "Love Story," "Forever & Always" (with fellow performer Joe Jonas as a captive audience) and "Change." The singer even manages an onstage costume change in a six-minute set, shedding her winter coat to reveal a black, sparkly Stephen Burrows dress. Taylor finishes off the set, like her year, on a high note, telling the crowd, "This is a new year, a new beginning, and things . . . will . . . change!"

★ Taylor is declared *CosmoGirl*'s Girl of the Year for 2008.

JANUARY 2009

★ Taylor makes her first appearance on *Saturday Night Live* as a musical guest. Taylor tells *Glamour*, "I got to meet Kristen Wiig and Andy Samberg, who are some of my favorite people."

FEBRUARY 2009

★ Tickets for the Fearless Tour go on sale and sell out completely minutes later.

★ Though Taylor didn't receive any Grammy noms, she still takes the stage with friend Miley Cyrus to perform "Fifteen."

★ Though she clarifies she's not a designer, Taylor collaborates on a line of L.e.i. sundresses available exclusively at Walmart, sharing her signature style with girls everywhere. Always mindful of her audience, Taylor keeps the price to $14, noting, "I never want to put my name on something that an 18-year-old girl struggling through her freshman year of college can't afford, or a family of four who won't spend $150 for a dress."

★ Taylor goes on a nine-day promotional tour in England, Scotland, and Germany.

★ *Jonas Brothers: The 3D Concert Experience* hits theaters nationwide, with Taylor joining the brothers onscreen to perform "Should've Said No."

MARCH 2009

★ The golden-haired beauty is given every musician's dream, a cover of *Rolling Stone.*

★ Taylor makes her acting debut on *CSI* on the March 5 episode, "Turn, Turn, Turn." The episode also features a remixed version of "You're Not Sorry."

★ *Rolling Stone* names Taylor one of the 100 people who are changing America. But ever-modest Taylor points out to Jay Leno that she was among scientists, neurosurgeons, and environmentalists and under their names they have "all these really technologically profound quotes about the essence of humanity." She adds, "And then you get to mine and it says Taylor Swift, quote: 'Today me and Miley ate a whole pizza in like five minutes!'"

★ On March 20, Taylor plays the Houston Rodeo to a massive crowd of 72,658 (the eighth largest crowd ever, outdoing even the Jonas Brothers by 183 people).

★ The soundtrack for *Hannah Montana: The Movie* is released on the 24th, which features Taylor Swift's "Crazier," a song she performs in the movie. When the filmmakers emailed her looking for "a song you could fall in love to," Taylor sent them "Crazier," and they fell in love with it. The song peaks at number 17 on the Hot 100 in May, and reaches number 28 on the Pop 100.

APRIL 2009

★ At the Academy of Country Music Awards, Taylor wins two major awards, Album of the Year and the Crystal

Milestone Award for selling more albums than anyone else that year. Astonished, Taylor remarks, "I write songs in my bedroom, and have so much fun doing this, it doesn't really feel like work. The fact that you can win Album of the Year for that was just unbelievable to me."

★ *Forbes* magazine gives Taylor the number four spot on their annual list of country music's top earners, estimating her annual take to be $18 million. She's also the highest-ranked female performer on the list.

★ In a major milestone moment, Taylor kicks off her first headlining tour on April 23 in Evansville, Indiana, where that date is declared Taylor Swift Day.

★ On the 27th, Taylor goes to class, Journalism 101, with her best friend Abigail at Kansas University. The superstar's presence doesn't go unnoticed. "It's funny how over the course of, like, an hour class that literally one text

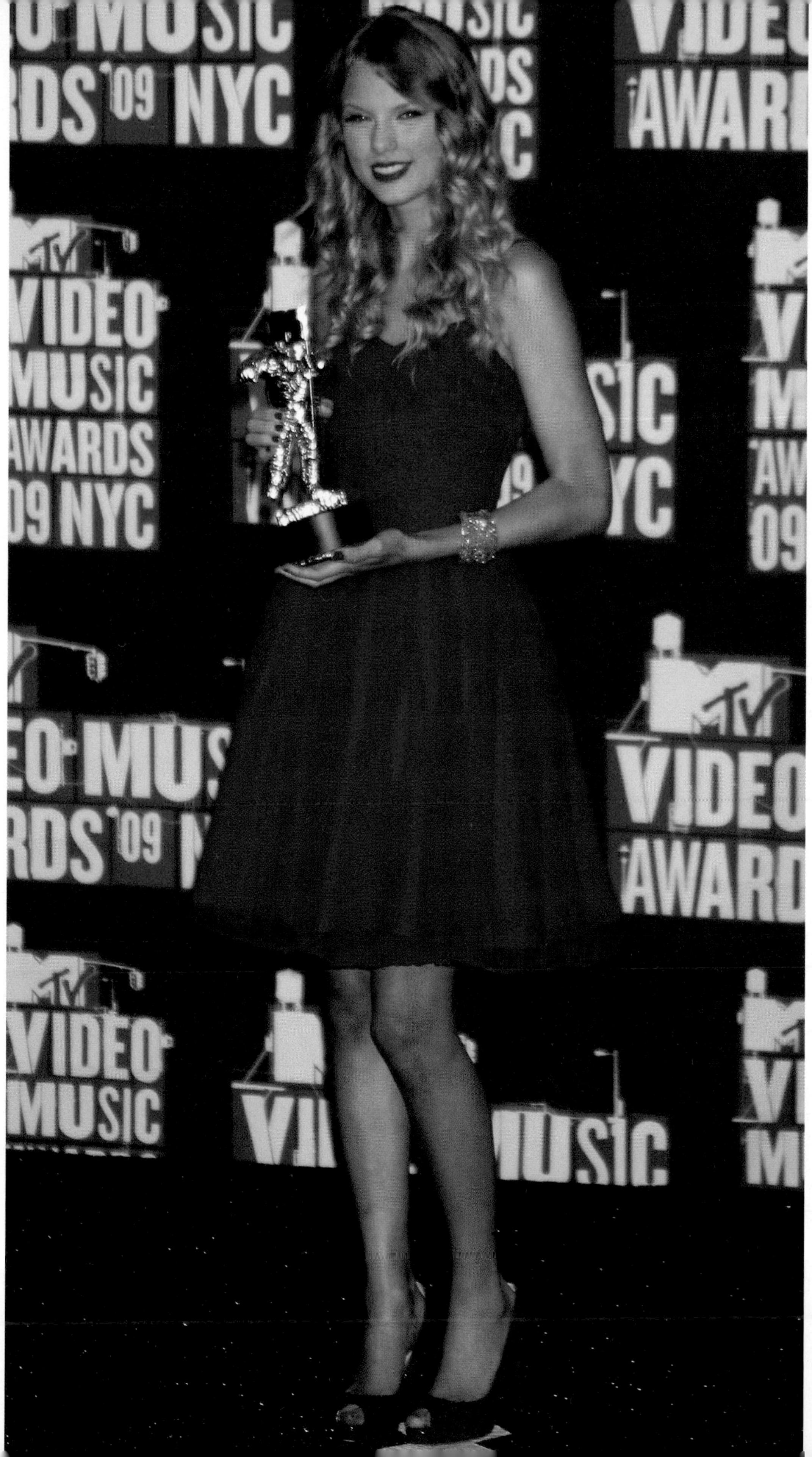
VIDEO
MUSIC
AWARDS
09 NYC

On September 13, 2009, Taylor was once again defying expectations as a country singer when she took to the stage to accept an MTV Video Music Award for her "You Belong with Me" video. But what happened next was even more unexpected. Just as she started her acceptance speech, rapper Kanye West stormed the stage, grabbing the mic from the astonished singer. He said, "Yo, Taylor, I'm really happy for you, I'll let you finish, but Beyoncé had one of the best videos of all time. One of the best videos of all time!" The camera cut to a shocked and appalled Beyoncé. When Kanye returned the microphone, Taylor stood there stunned and the audience gave her a supportive standing ovation. Sources at the VMAs reported that the 19-year-old burst into tears backstage. At the end of the night, when Beyoncé accepted her award for Video of the Year, she generously invited Taylor up on stage with her to give her the moment that had been stolen from her.

After the ceremony, Kanye's actions came under fire from everyone from average people to celebrities like Pink, Joel Madden of Good Charlotte, Perez Hilton, Katy Perry, and even President Barack Obama. Said Taylor, "I didn't expect anything like that could ever happen and I also didn't expect the support and love that came afterward." Later, Kanye posted a rambling apology on his blog, which was eventually replaced by a more humble admission: "That was Taylor's moment and I had no right in any way to take it from her." Though Kanye apologized publicly on *The Jay Leno Show*, it wasn't until Taylor's appearance on *The View*, that Kanye called personally to apologize. Taylor accepted the apology, and at least there was one consolation – it made for great material in her *Saturday Night Live* monologue.

message can set off a whole campus," said Abigail of the insta-crowd.

MAY 2009

★ "Fifteen" inspires a partnership with Best Buy called "@15." @15 is a "teen-led social change platform" that lets teens decide where Best Buy's charitable donations should go. @15 is the official charitable partner of the Fearless Tour, and Taylor recorded a "Teen Service Announcement" that plays at each stop on her North American tour. Before each show, Taylor donates 40 free tickets and an autographed Taylor guitar to teen-focused charities like the YMCA, the Boys and Girls club, and Big Brothers/Big Sisters.

★ On the 31st, Taylor's *Dateline* special airs. The show goes behind the scenes in the lead-up to the Fearless Tour's launch, revealing a grounded, hard-working young woman, unanimously adored by friends, coworkers, and fans.

JUNE 2009

★ Proving she can rap like the best of the shorties in extra-small white Ts, Taylor films a segment for the CMT Music Awards with T-Pain, poking fun at her good-girl persona in "Thug Story."

★ At the CMT Music Awards ceremony, Taylor wins the fan-voted Video of the Year and Female Video of the Year awards. She writes to her fans to thank them in "A driving-home-wondering-how-on-earth-you-got-so-lucky-and-semi-questioning-whether-you-just-

hallucinated-the-whole-night kind of way."

AUGUST 2009

★ Taylor surfs to victory with teen voters, earning Teen Choice Awards for Choice Female Album and Choice Female Artist.

★ On August 27, Taylor plays her sold-out-in-one-minute show at Madison Square Garden, and afterward tweets, "Most. Amazing. Night. That's what I'll look back on when I'm old."

OCTOBER 2009

★ After filming some romantic scenes over the summer with Twilight heartthrob Taylor Lautner for *Valentine's Day*, rumors start to really heat up about a Taylor and Taylor power pairing when the two are spotted hanging out. Neither Taylor officially confirms a relationship.

★ Tickets for the 2010 leg of the Fearless Tour go on sale on October 23, and 15 shows sell out within minutes.

★ On October 26, a day before the album's scheduled on-sale date, Taylor releases what she jokingly calls the "Fearless Jedi Ninja Platinum Edition," otherwise known as *Fearless: Platinum Edition*. It doesn't come with Wookies or nunchucks, but it does come with six new tracks, her videos, behind-the-scenes featurettes, and great photos by her brother Austin. He was invited to be the tour photographer after getting a new camera and snapping some stunning pics.

★ Taylor receives some love from her hometown at the Nashville Music Awards when she's named Artist of the Year, Songwriter/Artist of the Year, and awarded Album of the Year for *Fearless*.

NOVEMBER 2009

★ With the release of *Band Hero* on the 3rd, anyone can try their hand at being Taylor. Taylor is featured in the *Band Hero* commercial with musicians she admires: Travis Barker, Pete Wentz, and Rivers Cuomo.

★ On November 5, Taylor Guitars releases a Taylor Swift guitar that's three-quarter sized, and has vines and the songstress's signature around the sound hole. The guitar reminds the singer of her early days on the road. "I used to sit in the back seat of the rental car while I was on my radio tour at 16, writing songs on my Baby Taylor guitar," said Taylor. "I love the sound, and I love those memories."

★ Taylor makes her return to *Saturday Night Live* on the 7th, this time as host and musical guest. The young star is the first country singer to host the show since one of her idols, Dolly Parton, in 1989.

★ On John Mayer's album *Battle Studies*, Taylor sings on the track "Half of My Heart." A long-time fan of Mayer's music, Taylor was excited "about just the idea that he would even mention me in his Twitter," let alone that she'd sing a duet with him.

★ Exactly one year after she released *Fearless*, Taylor Swift has another night to remember, when she not only earns Album of the Year at the Country Music Association Awards for her sophomore effort, but also makes history as the youngest person to win the prestigious Entertainer of the Year award. That night, Taylor sweeps her nominations, turning all five into coveted crystal statuettes.

★ At the American Music Awards on the 22nd, Taylor wins Artist of the Year. Though Taylor only appears at the awards via satellite from London, she earns five AMAs by the end of the evening.

★ Live on British television, Taylor donates £13,000 to Children in Need.

★ Though country music is a hard sell overseas, on November 23, Taylor plays for 12,500 British fans at London's Wembley Arena, where, the *Telegraph* noted, "she reinforced her status as every young girl's best friend." Taylor follows with a second show in Manchester on November 24.

DECEMBER 2009

★ To celebrate turning the big 2-0 and another year of unimaginable achievement, Taylor throws herself a Christmas-themed birthday party with her friends, band, and tour crew at her home in Hendersonville. This year the songwriter *gives* gifts on her birthday instead of just receiving them — she donates $250,000 to the various schools she attended. "Something I wanted to do at the end of this amazing year and especially on my birthday was give back to something I really believe in, which is education," she said. "The schools that I went to and the amazing people I got to learn from really turned me into who I am, and I wanted to give back."

★ Taylor performs at the Z100 Jingle Ball in NYC with other musical sensations like Ke$ha, John Mayer, Justin Bieber, and Jordin Sparks. Taylor tweeted about the night: "Tonight was one of those nights you don't ever forget the details of. Every little thing was shiny. Jingle Ball. What a way to end the year."

★ After a year of unprecedented success, Taylor is the cover girl for *People*'s 25 most intriguing people of 2009 issue. Her company on the list includes Brad Pitt and Angelina Jolie, Sandra Bullock, Neil Patrick Harris, Barack and Michelle Obama, Rihanna, and Sarah Palin.

★ Following in the footsteps of Stephen Colbert and Tina Fey, Taylor is named AP Entertainer of the Year. "I am so honored and excited," says Taylor. "This was so unexpected, and I could not be more grateful." Other end-of-the-year honors include being named MTV News' number two Woman of the Year and *Billboard*'s Artist of the Year, with its editors praising her as "a graceful, timeless celebrity" on a swift ascent to the top.

JANUARY 2010

★ Once again, the Taylor Nation shows support for their cherished singer-songwriter, and Taylor takes home the People's Choice Award for Favorite Female Artist.

★ Just 10 days after a devastating earthquake struck Haiti on January 12, Taylor joins an all-star roster for the Hope for Haiti Now global benefit, donating her time to answer phones, as well as performing a cover of Better Than Ezra's "Breathless." "I've never actually worked a phone bank before," Taylor said. "But I want to do everything I can to help out this horrible situation. I'm passionate about this. This one was an immediate yes." A recording of her performance was made available on iTunes, with all proceeds going to non-profit associations working in Haiti.

★ On the 19th, Taylor releases "Today Was a Fairytale" for digital download, and it debuts at number two on the Billboard Hot 100, making it her highest debut ever. It has 325,000 downloads in its first week alone, breaking the record for first week sales by a female artist previously held by Britney Spears for "Womanizer."

★ Nashville's princess becomes the Queen of iPods as the highest-selling digital artist in history with 24.3 million downloads.

★ On the 31st, Taylor performs at the Grammy Awards with rock legend Stevie Nicks. Her performance that night comes under fire from the media, but Taylor still has reason to walk away standing tall with four Grammys — Best Country Vocal Performance, Best Country Song, Best Country Album and Album of the Year.

Taylor and Faith Hill at a charity event for the Entertainment Industry Foundation's Women's Cancer Research Fund.

FEBRUARY 2010

★ On February 12, Taylor makes her acting debut on the silver screen in the ensemble romantic comedy *Valentine's Day*.

★ Just in time for Valentine's Day, Taylor's line of 12 greeting cards with American Greetings is officially available in stores. "Taylor's songs touch millions of people and we believe her cards will have the same emotional appeal . . . we are very excited for everyone to experience them," said American Greetings exec Kelly Ricker.

★ Taylor is nominated for two 2010 Kids' Choice Awards — Favorite Female Singer and Favorite Song for "You Belong with Me."

MARCH 2010

★ Taylor is nominated for four major ACM Awards — Top Female Vocalist, Video of the Year and Song of the Year (for "You Belong with Me"), and Entertainer of the Year.

★ Big Machine releases a free Taylor Swift iPhone application, so "any time Taylor releases new music, videos, or photos (and more), fans will be instantly updated directly on their iPhones."

As Andrea Swift (right) looks on, Liz Rose embraces Taylor as she reacts to winning her very first Grammy.

APRIL 2010

★ Taylor graces the cover of *Elle*'s April issue not just once but twice. One cover features Taylor in a black leather jacket; the other in a signature silver sparkly dress. Says Taylor in the interview, "I like to categorize the various levels of heartbreak. I've only had that happen once. A letdown is worth a few songs. A heartbreak is worth a few albums."

★ At the ACM Awards on the 18th, Taylor performs "Change," and changes her costume halfway through the song. For the rousing finish, Taylor is accompanied by the Tritones, an a cappella group from the University of California, San Diego, then dives into the crowd!

★ Taylor announces that she'll be the newest easy, breezy, beautiful CoverGirl, with a cosmetics campaign debuting in January 2011. Also in April, Taylor's ads for the Sony CyberShot Camera air.

MAY 2010

★ Taylor is part of the all-star ACM concert special *Brooks & Dunn:*

The Last Rodeo on the 23rd, with musical guests such as Keith Urban, Carrie Underwood, Reba McEntire, Rascal Flatts, and Brad Paisley.

★ Taylor donates $500,000 to Nashville flood relief. "Being at home during the storm, I honestly could not believe what was happening to the city and the people I love so dearly," Taylor wrote in an email. "Nashville is my home, and the reason why I get to do what I love. I have always been proud to be a Nashvillian, but especially now, seeing the love that runs through this city when there are people in crisis."

★ In the May issue of *Vogue*, Taylor talks about how unbelievable her life is: "Looking back on what these past two years have been for me, it feels like this magical dream of 'Really? We toured all over the world? We played an arena in London? This is happening?' Readjusting my goals and dreams has been something I've had to do a lot lately."

★ Taylor glams up and attends the Met Costume Institute gala on the 3rd in a shimmering beaded white Ralph Lauren gown.

★ "Love Story" earns Taylor a BMI Pop Award for Song of the Year.

JUNE 2010

★ Putting her lucky number to the test, Taylor does a 13-hour meet-and-greet on the 13th at the Bridgestone Arena in Nashville. From 8 a.m. to 9 p.m., Taylor hangs out with fans and also performs a short acoustic set.

★ The 41st Annual Songwriters Hall of Fame ceremony takes place and Taylor receives an award and performs.

★ After the disastrous floods, Taylor takes the stage on the 23rd for Nashville Rising: A Benefit Concert for Flood Recovery.

JULY 2010

★ Fans finally get the news they've been waiting for: Tay hosts a live chat to announce that her new album *Speak Now* comes out on October 25th.

AUGUST 2010

★ Taylor's first single "Mine" gets a video, which debuts on the 24th, and Taylor performs the song in Kennebunk, Maine, where she shot the video.

SEPTEMBER 2010

★ Taylor kicks off the month at the CMA Music Fest where she performs "Mine."

★ Football and Swifty? Taylor has a pigskin double-header, attending a game at brother Austin's college, Notre Dame, with Selena Gomez before performing "Mine" at the NFL Opening Kickoff a few days later.

★ With Kanye West in the audience of the MTV Video Music Awards, Taylor performs "Innocent" at the site of the infamous interruption on the 12th.

★ Taylor joins country stars for the "All For the Hall" event to fundraise for the Country Music Hall of Fame and Museum in Nashville.

★ Taylor attends the Roberto Cavalli

heads to a Starbucks and a Target in New York City to buy her album. She also surprises fans with a free concert in Central Park.

★ Taylor comes face to face with herself . . . or at least the wax version, when Madame Tussaud's unveils their newest celeb stand-in in New York. The figure wears a Jenny Packham dress (and Taylor dresses to match) and carries a custom-made version of "Sparkles," complete with 2,000 Swarovski crystals.

★ Taylor encourages kids to read by performing at the Read Now! event held for school students and hosted by Nick Cannon. Her New York promotional tour continues with a short concert at JFK Airport as part of Jet Blue's concert series.

★ West Coast fans get their own surprise show when Taylor does a set on Hollywood Boulevard. Her performances of "Mine" and "Long Live" atop a double-decker bus pop up on NBC's Thanksgiving special.

NOVEMBER 2010

★ Elizabeth Arden announces a fragrance deal with the Sparkly One. Says Taylor, "I have always loved how fragrance can shape a memory the way certain scents remind you of events and people that are imprinted in your thoughts."

★ All of Taylor's hard work to promote the album pays off when first-week sales of *Speak Now* hit 1,044,477, giving her a number-one debut.

★ Taylor hits the stage of *Dancing with the*

fashion shows in Milan and Paris; she later wears the designer's work during the Speak Now Tour.

OCTOBER 2010

★ Taylor hits the Second Annual CMA Songwriters Luncheon in Nashville, where she is honored with the Triple Play Award for her songs "Should've Said No," "Love Story," and "White Horse."

★ The release of *Speak Now* on the 27th means a media whirlwind month for Taylor. The day her album drops, Taylor

Stars to perform "Mine" and "White Horse."

★ Taylor Swift breaks another record, becoming the first artist to have 11 songs on the Billboard Hot 100 chart at the same time from the same album, and the only female artist to ever have that many songs on the chart simultaneously.

★ For the third year in a row, Tay picks up Songwriter of the Year at the BMI Country Music Awards.

★ Taylor plays the grand piano in a stunning performance of "Back to December" (complete with snow) at the Country Music Awards.

★ Across the pond, Taylor performs three songs at the BBC Radio 1's Teen Awards: "Love Story," "Speak Now," and "Mine."

★ Taylor's award shelf gets a little more crowded when she wins Favorite Country Female Artist at the American Music Awards for third time in a row. She also performs her mash-up of "Back to December"/"Apologize." After the show, Taylor tweets, "Thank you for the AMA. I'm so thrilled and thankful. I'm so excited, I think you've cured my jet lag!"

★ International fans are thrilled when Taylor announces her Speak Now World Tour dates.

★ Turkey and Taylor! NBC airs its *Taylor Swift: Speak Now* Thanksgiving special on the 25th.

DECEMBER 2010

★ On the 3rd, Taylor is honored as one of CMT's Artists of the Year along with Jason Aldean, Lady Antebellum, Carrie

Underwood, and the Zac Brown Band. Taylor writes about how awesome the event was to attend, saying, "There were loving, 'so happy to see you again' hugs given, and we got to watch some reeeeally cool performances."

★ E! airs its special about Taylor, featuring interviews with Andrea Swift among others in the know.

★ It's no surprise to Swifties that *Speak Now* is certified triple platinum less than two months after its release.

★ Taylor hits Manhattan to launch her

NatureLuxe CoverGirl campaign with events and interviews.

★ Pop artist Peter Max, who has also painted numerous presidents, musicians, sports heroes, and other pop icons, gives Taylor an awesome birthday gift: a psychedelic painting of her *Speak Now* album cover. (He brought *Fearless* to the canvas earlier in 2010, and one of his four Swifty portraits now hangs in Taylor's Nashville pad.) "She is one of the most beautiful and talented stars we have today," says Peter.

★ On the 13th, Tay celebrates her 21st birthday. The highlight? "When my brother walked through the door in the middle of the party. He's away at college and I didn't think I'd see him until Christmas! But there he was, walking through the door with his backpack. I was SO surprised!"

★ *Entertainment Weekly* crowns Taylor "Entertainer of the Year," making her the youngest person to ever receive the honor. Taylor follows in the footsteps of people she adores like Ellen DeGeneres (1997) and the cast of *Grey's Anatomy* (2006).

JANUARY 2011

★ Taylor starts the year at number one, with *Speak Now* topping the Billboard 200 again.

★ Easy, breezy, beautiful Taylor is featured in a new CoverGirl campaign, and she celebrates the brand's 50th anniversary in Hollywood on the 5th, striking hilarious poses on the red carpet with fellow CoverGirl Ellen Degeneres.

- ★ At the People's Choice Awards, Taylor wins Favorite Country Artist and presents Favorite Movie Actor to Johnny Depp.
- ★ More accolades roll in for Taylor from her success in 2010: she's named Billboard and Nielsen SoundScan's top-selling artist of the year for the second time in three years, as well as Billboard's most-played artist, for the second year in a row. And with over 34 million tracks sold to date, Taylor holds on to her number-one position atop Billboard's chart of Top Selling Digital Artists in music history.
- ★ The melancholy music video for "Back to December" debuts on the 13th.
- ★ As her world tour approaches, Taylor plays a show on board the cruise ship *Allure of the Seas*.
- ★ Taylor pauses her tour prep to celebrate with family, friends, and industry at the Hard Rock Café in Nashville on the 28th, where she receives awards for the number-one success of her "Mine" single and video and a plaque from the Recording Industry Association of America commemorating total shipments of more than 13 million records.

FEBRUARY 2011

- ★ On the 9th, Taylor hits the stage in Singapore to kick off the Asian leg of the Speak Now World Tour.
- ★ It's Oscars season, and Taylor attends a few parties with Emma Stone including the *Vanity Fair* post-show party along with pal Ashley Avignone.

MARCH 2011

- ★ News breaks that Taylor will be joining the voice cast of *Dr. Seuss' The Lorax*, along with Zac Efron, Ed Helms, and Danny DeVito.
- ★ While in the U.K. for her Speak Now Tour, Taylor records a BBC Radio 1 Live Lounge session, doing acoustic versions of "The Story of Us," and covering "White Blank Page" by Mumford & Sons. She also performs an exclusive 10-song set at BBC Radio 2, live from the legendary Abbey Road Studios.
- ★ Taylor Swift ends her European tour on a celebratory note: she reaches the 20 million mark in worldwide album sales.

APRIL 2011

- ★ At the 46th Annual Academy of Country Music Awards, Taylor performs "Mean," and while she doesn't win Album of the Year or Female Vocalist, she takes home the big one: Entertainer of the Year.
- ★ Taylor adds to her real estate portfolio with a west coast pad in L.A. The cozy country cottage allows Taylor a break from hotels when she's in the City of Angels. The same month, the grateful daughter also buys her parents a new $1.4 million home in Nashville.
- ★ On the 22nd, Taylor's debut album, *Taylor Swift*, officially sells over 5 million copies in the U.S., making her the second female country artist to do this with two or more albums.
- ★ When Taylor's Facebook page hits 20 million likes, she posts "to say hi and

thanks SO SO SO much. . . . I love you like woah. A lot."

MAY 2011

★ Taylor starts the month in Manhattan attending the Met's Costume Institute gala, wearing a J. Mendel dress.

★ To raise money for tornado disaster relief in the southeast states, Taylor decides to make her final tour rehearsal a benefit concert. "I was watching the coverage of the tornadoes backstage at rehearsals," said the singer, "and I wanted to do something for the families affected by the damage. I've never opened a rehearsal to the public before, but I felt that inviting my fans to the last rehearsal for the Speak Now Tour would be a great way to raise money." With 13,000 tickets sold plus merchandise, Taylor swiftly raises well over $750,000 with her "Speak Now . . . Help Now" concert on May 21.

★ At the Billboard Music Awards, Taylor nabs three awards — Top Billboard 200 Album, Top Country Album, and Top Country Artist — and also introduces Nicki Minaj's performance.

★ In a banner month, the superstar releases two videos, with "Mean" debuting on CMT and "The Story of Us" on MTV.

JUNE 2011

★ At the CMT Music Awards, which Taylor misses due to a tour date, she wins Video of the Year for "Mine." Despite her absence, Tay finds a way to be a part of the show with a pre-recorded video where she plays Thelma to Shania Twain's Louise.

★ Taylor has the honor of closing CMA's four-day festival with a performance at the LP Field in Nashville.

★ Putting her money where her heart is, Taylor donates $50,000 to St. Jude Children's Research Hospital.

★ In a post on Taylor Connect, Taylor updates fans about the tour: "I should just tell you up front that playing shows on this tour is the best time I've ever had onstage. The crowds we've been playing for have been so unbelievable. The kind of crowds that jump up and down the entire show, making our view from the stage look like a giant ocean of dancing, jumping people. These are the kinds of crowds that sing the words louder and more passionately than I ever could've imagined."

JULY 2011

★ For the first time in her career, Taylor has to cancel shows thanks to a nasty case of bronchitis. Taylor tweets an apology to Louisville, saying it's her "first time having to do this. I'm so, so sorry." Her shows in Charlotte and Atlanta are also rescheduled.

AUGUST 2011

★ Though she's no longer a teen herself, the teens of America still choose Taylor, and she picks up six awards at the TCAs on the 7th.

★ Thanks to Taylor's tornado relief benefit, she wins a Do Something Award from VH1.com.

★ With a few days off, Taylor decides to take the girls on her tour (band members, dancers, and aerialists) on mini-vacay in South Carolina where they kick up their heels (and some sand on the beach) on their first proper break since the tour started in February.

SEPTEMBER 2011

★ Taylor sits down for a Q&A session with YouTube, her first long interview (clocking in at 42 minutes) in a while.

★ At a Rodarte show during New York fashion week, Taylor is seated in the front row next to *Vogue*'s Anna Wintour.

★ At the 5th Annual ACM Honors show in Nashville on the 19th, Taylor receives the Jim Reeves International Award, "for outstanding contributions to the acceptance of country music throughout the world."

OCTOBER 2011

★ Taylor is honored at the 41st Nashville Songwriters Hall of Fame event as songwriter/artist of the year, and she performs an Alan Jackson song, "Where Were You (When the World Stopped Turning)."

★ What does a Taylor Swift song smell like? Well, according to her signature scent, Wonderstruck, released with Elizabeth Arden, "Enchanted" is floral and fruity notes on a wooden background. Smell can be an important part of that first moment of falling, and Taylor enthuses, "A fragrance can help shape someone's first impression and

memory of you, and it's exciting to think that Wonderstruck will play a role in creating some of those memories." Eau de T-Swizzle becomes the second-bestselling fragrance of the 2011 holiday season.

★ On the anniversary of *Speak Now*'s release, Taylor writes to her fans to thank them: "You guys have done so many wonderful things to make this year so magical, and I can't thank you enough. I remember this week last year being one of the busiest and most exciting weeks of my life. It was the end of this week last year that I got the call that told me you guys had gone out and bought over a MILLION copies of *Speak Now*. I'm just sitting here in my dressing room reminiscing. I'm so lucky to have you in my life. Thank you for a wonderful year."

NOVEMBER 2011

★ At the BMI Country Awards, which celebrates songwriters and music publishers, Taylor gets some love for "Fearless," "Mine," and "Back to December."

★ Taylor takes Entertainer of the Year honors for the second time at the CMA Awards on 9th. She also takes to the stage and performs "Ours."

★ *60 Minutes* airs an in-depth profile of Taylor by Leslie Stahl.

★ At the American Music Awards, Taylor looks like she has a great time sitting next to bestie Selena and winning Favorite Country Female Artist, Favorite Country Album, and Artist of the Year.

★ Fans who couldn't get Swifty tickets in the minute before they sold out get to share in the concert experience with the release of *Speak Now World Tour Live* as an album and a DVD. The album enters the Hot 200 at number 11 and number 2 on the Billboard Country Albums chart.

★ On the 23rd, Taylor and company wrap up the North American leg of the Speak Now Tour with two shows at Madison Square Garden featuring surprise guests Goo Goo Dolls, Selena Gomez, and James Taylor.

★ Faith Hill presents Taylor with her CMT Artists of the Year award.

DECEMBER 2011

★ Billboard names Taylor "Woman of the Year," making her the youngest artist ever to receive the honor.

★ Taylor announces that she'll be contributing to *The Hunger Games* soundtrack. Instead of drawing on her own experiences, the songwriter adopts a new point-of-view: "When the Hunger Games people came to me and said, 'We want you to write from Katniss's perspective,' it was really crazy to read that book, jump into her skin, and to have a whole different set of hopes and fears in front of me."

★ *Forbes* names Taylor the highest-earning star under 30, and *Billboard* hails Taylor as the Country Artist of 2011.

JANUARY 2012

★ Taylor wins Favorite Country Artist at the PCAs but doesn't attend.

★ Taylor pops up onstage during The Civil Wars' show at the Ryman Auditorium in Nashville on the 13th to sing "Safe and Sound."

★ Supporting her favorite Kennedy, Taylor attends the premiere of the documentary *Ethel* at the Sundance Film Festival in Park City, Utah, on the 20th.

★ Taylor makes a visit to the Ronald McDonald House of New York, where she gives an acoustic performance and signs autographs for sick children.

FEBRUARY 2012

★ Taylor covers *Vogue* for their February issue.

★ Taylor joins the National Education Association's Read Across America Day, on the 2nd, to motivate children and teens to read.

★ At the Grammys on the 12th, Taylor

knocks it out of the park with her performance of "Mean" and wins Best Country Song and Best Country Solo Performance for the song.

★ Taylor hits the orange carpet at the Hollywood world premiere of *The Lorax*, which becomes a box-office smash. As part of the movie promotional tour, she and Zac Efron visit *Ellen*, where they sing their own version of "Pumped Up Kicks" by Foster the People.

MARCH 2012

★ *Billboard* names the Top 40 Money Makers in music, and Taylor lands another number one.

★ Though Taylor sings about breaking up a wedding in "Speak Now," Justin Bieber reduces her to tears when he makes her believe she'd ruined one by setting off a firecracker: luckily, no weddings were harmed, but Taylor Swift was officially *Punk'd*.

★ At the Kids' Choice Awards on 31st, Taylor wins the Big Help Award, which is presented to her by First Lady Michelle Obama.

APRIL 2012

★ Taylor kicks off the month at the ACM Awards, where she takes home Entertainer of the Year for the second year in a row.

★ In support of the American Red Cross, Taylor auctions off tickets to her Ottawa concert.

MAY 2012

★ "Mean" gets the *Glee* treatment during its episode on the 16th.

★ Taylor donates $4 million to the Country Music Hall of Fame and Museum in Nashville. The Taylor Swift Education Center, set to open in early 2014, will feature an exhibition and classroom space. "Her love for the museum is well documented," said a spokesperson. "One of her first public performances was in the museum's plaza, and she held a ceremony to sign her recording contract at the institution."

JUNE 2012

★ *Rolling Stone* places Taylor at number 45 on their "Women Who Rock" list, praising her as "one of the few genuine rock stars we've got these days, with a flawless ear for what makes a song click."

★ Swifty performs at the Walmart Shareholder Meeting, where she's interviewed by Justin Timberlake.

★ The "Taylor Swift: Speak Now — Treasures from the World Tour" exhibit opens at the Country Music Hall of Fame and Museum, with Scott and Andrea Swift, and her brother, Austin, at the opening event. The exhibit runs from June 6th to November 4th.

★ Taylor Swift is awarded the 2012 Honorary Star of Compassion Award by Northwest Tennessee Disaster Services, a Tennessee nonprofit group dedicated to disaster relief and education.

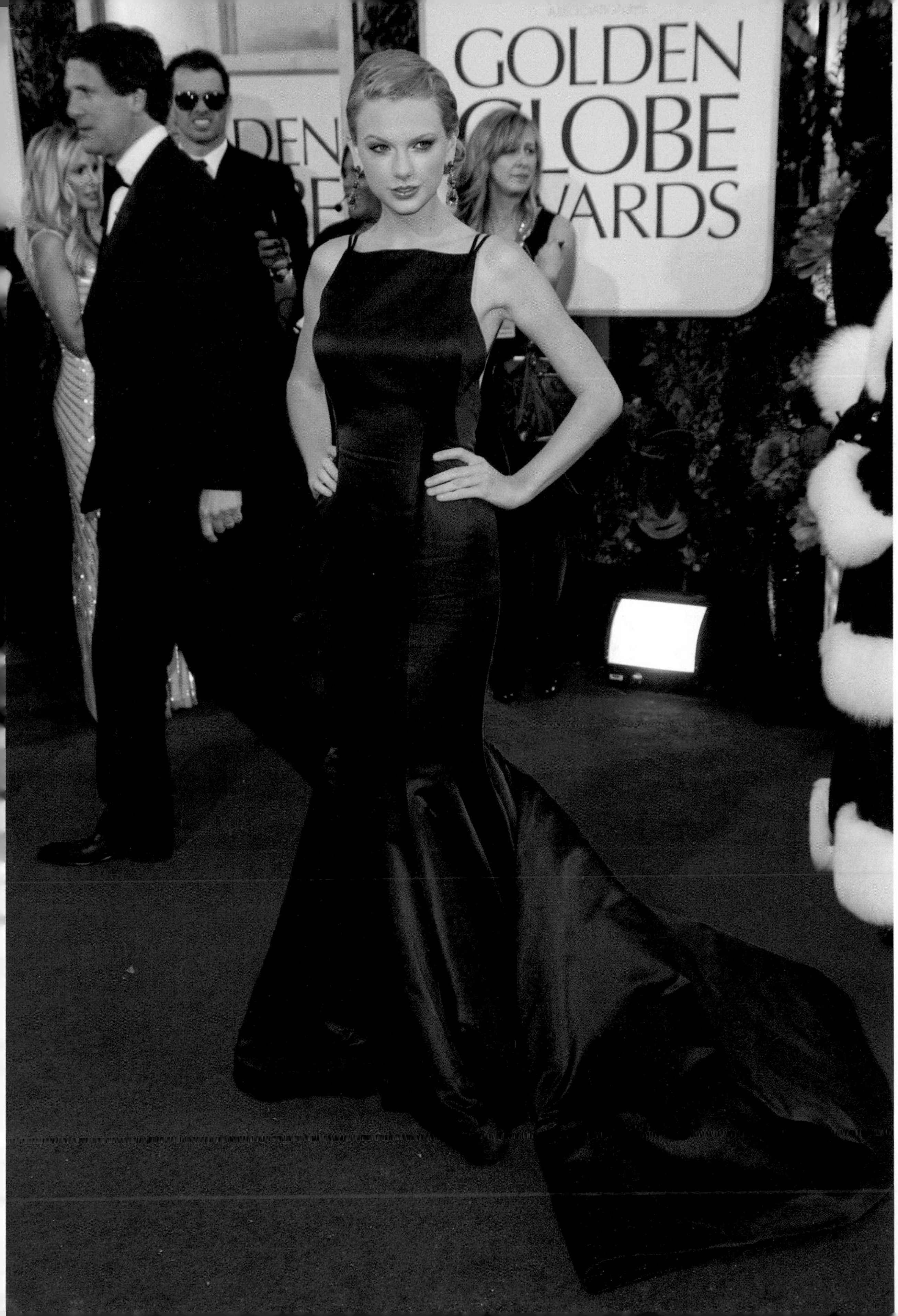
GOLDEN

about everybody really." In an interview with the *Guardian*, Taylor says, "One of the things people don't really recognize about the similarities between country and hip-hop is that they're celebrations of pride in a lifestyle."

JULY 2012

★ On the 3rd, Taylor makes a surprise appearance onstage with James Taylor during his concert in Massachusetts.

★ A new Elizabeth Arden Wonderstruck commercial debuts with Taylor explaining that "Wonderstruck is about that moment when you instantly feel a connection to someone, but then there's that feeling of being completely enamored — enchanted — when you know a little more about that someone and still feel that strong connection."

★ At the Teen Choice Awards on the 22nd, Tay takes home five surfboards and dances in the audience. Asked about her dance moves, Taylor says, "I just, like, practice actively not caring what I look like! So I think half of dancing to stuff is not being self-conscious because I am not a good dancer but I do dance!"

AUGUST 2012

★ Taylor participates in a PSA for Fashion's Night Out, encouraging people to buy the FNO tee that benefits the New York City AIDS Fund.

★ Taylor gets her first number one on the Billboard Hot 100 with "We Are Never Ever Getting Back Together" with 623,000 downloads, the most for a

★ Though Taylor has three nominations at the CMT Music Awards on the 6th, she goes home without hardware.

★ The video for B.o.B.'s "Both of Us" debuts. The two braved bugs and spiders to film the video in Nashville, which is directed by Jake Nava. B.o.B. says of "Both of Us," "The song is more like a project, this is bigger than just B.o.B. and Taylor Swift. This is about all walks of life, all classes of society. It's

female artist in a single week. The lead single's video debuts on the 30th.

SEPTEMBER 2012

★ Taylor performs "We Are Never Ever Getting Back Together" at the MTV Video Music Awards on the 6th.

★ On the 7th, Taylor performs at the Stand Up to Cancer concert, singing "Ronan" about a four-year-old boy who died from neuroblastoma. Taylor wrote the song after reading his mother's blog; Maya is credited as a co-writer of the song. Released as a single, the song debuts at number two on the Digital Songs chart with all proceeds going to cancer charities.

★ Taylor attends the 2012 Canadian Country Music Association Awards on the 9th in Saskatoon, Canada, to receive the Generation Award in celebration of her global success.

★ Taylor's hectic schedule takes her to Brazil, where the tireless singer does a round of promotional interviews as well as a concert at Citibank Hall in Rio de Janeiro on the 13th.

OCTOBER 2012

★ Taylor starts the month in Paris, where she attends Fashion Week and films her video for "Begin Again" before hitting London.

★ Walgreens announces it's launching a Taylor Swift merchandise line in time for the holiday season.

★ Taylor covers *Rolling Stone* for its October issue.

★ Everyone's seeing *Red* as Taylor goes into promo frenzy mode in advance of the album's release on the 22nd.

★ "I Knew You Were Trouble" becomes Taylor's 50th song to crack the Billboard 100.

★ Taylor's lucky number the week after her album drops isn't 13, but 1,209,817 — the number of copies she has sold of *Red* in one week.

★ For those who want to sport red from head-to-toe, Taylor partners with classic shoemaker Keds to release a limited edition pair of red kicks the same week she releases her album.

★ Taylor scores her first number-one debut in the U.K. when *Red* tops the album charts upon its release.

★ Wearing a red bow tie, polka-dot shirt, shorts, and ponytail, Taylor performs "We Are Never Ever Getting Back Together" on *Dancing with the Stars* on the 30th.

★ *Red* earns the biggest sales week for any album in over a decade, with two copies of *Red* sold every second in the second last week of the month in the U.S.

NOVEMBER 2012

★ Taylor opens the CMAs with "Begin Again," but doesn't take home any awards. Taylor joins other celebs like Justin Bieber and Martha Stewart in a *Miracle on 34th Street*–themed Macy's Christmas commercial promoting Make-A-Wish donations.

★ Taylor embarks on a promotional tour to Europe. The poor girl has a cold but

soldiers on with performances and interviews.

★ Taylor closes the European Music Awards show with a circus-themed performance of "Never Ever" and wins three awards.

★ Taylor's episode of VH1's *Storytellers*, filmed at Harvey Mudd College in Claremont, California, airs on the 11th.

★ Tickets to the Red Tour sell out in minutes, proving that fans are hungry for more Taylor.

★ Noted fashion photographer Nigel Barker teams with Sony and Taylor for *8 Hours with Taylor Swift*, a photo book that comes with the purchase of certain Sony cameras.

★ Taylor performs "State of Grace" on *The X-Factor*, and loose-lipped judge Mario Lopez starts serious Harry Styles romance rumors.

★ At the AMAs, Taylor performs "I Knew You Were Trouble" and picks up the award for Favorite Country Female.

★ The busy Swift One heads from a promotional tour in Japan to Australia, where she promotes *Red* and sings "I Knew You Were Trouble" at the ARIA Awards.

DECEMBER 2012

★ *Forbes* names Taylor the seventh-highest-earning artist of the year (tied with Paul

McCartney), thanks to her music earnings, perfume, and cosmetics endorsements.

★ At the annual Z100 Jingle Ball, Taylor busts out some duets, performing "Everything Has Changed" with Ed Sheeran and "Both of Us" with B.o.B.

★ Tay's *Red* lands on *Rolling Stone*'s list of top albums of the year, with the influential magazine writing that the album is "a deepening and accentuating of Swift's natural gifts for storytelling and irrefutable hooks."

★ The Robert F. Kennedy Center for Justice and Human Rights gives Taylor the Ripple of Hope Award, which recognizes individuals who demonstrate commitment to social change.

★ Live from Nashville, Taylor co-hosts the Grammy Nominations Concert with LL Cool J on the 5th.

★ Taylor celebrates her birthday with a gift to her fans, releasing the "I Knew You Were Trouble" video, but Taylor gets a surprise gift herself: a Golden Globe nomination for "Safe and Sound."

★ It's announced that Taylor will appear on labelmate Tim McGraw's 2013 album *Two Lanes of Freedom*; Tim releases his track listing on December 13th, and Taylor appears on the 13th track, "Highway Don't Care," along with Keith Urban.

★ DoSomething.org names Taylor as the number-one celebrity do-gooder of the year.

★ Taylor rings in the new year in Times Square, performing "We Are Never Ever Getting Back Together" and "I Knew You Were Trouble" on Dick Clark's Rockin' New Year's Eve; at midnight, she shares a smooch with One Direction's Harry Styles.

★ Looking back on 2012 with ET, Taylor names her proudest moment as getting a standing ovation after performing "Mean" at the Grammys.

JANUARY 2013

★ A vision in white, Taylor takes home Favorite Country Artist and presents the award for Favorite Movie at the People's Choice Awards on the 9th.

★ Taylor attends the Golden Globes as a nominee for "Safe and Sound," but Adele takes home the honor for her James Bond theme song, "Skyfall."

★ Thanks to Taylor's smash hit "I Knew You Were Trouble," she becomes the first artist since the Beatles to spend six weeks or more at number one on the Billboard charts with three consecutive studio albums.

★ The latest in a Disney Dream Portraits campaign, Taylor's photos as Rapunzel, taken by the legendary Annie Leibovitz, are unveiled.

★ Taylor announces a new partnership with "one of the great loves of [her] life": Diet Coke.

★ The RIAA releases its 2012 stats, and with the success of *Red*, Taylor earns the year's highest album certification. She scores triple-platinum certification for "We Are Never Ever Getting Back Together," while "Red," "I Knew You Were Trouble," "Begin Again," and "Eyes

THE RED SET LIST

The Red Tour kicked off on 3/13/13 with this set list:

1. "State of Grace"
2. "Holy Ground"
3. "Red"
4. "You Belong with Me"
5. "The Lucky One"
6. "Mean"
7. "Stay Stay Stay"
8. "22"
9. "I Almost Do"
10. "Everything Has Changed"
11. "Begin Again"
12. "Sparks Fly"
13. "I Knew You Were Trouble"
14. "All Too Well"
15. "Love Story"
16. "Treacherous"
17. "We Are Never Ever Getting Back Together"

Open" each hit platinum status. Taylor's digital RIAA song certifications surpass 37 million sold since 2006.

★ Taylor does a promotional tour of Europe, which includes presenting at the NRJ Awards in Cannes.

★ Taylor's "Bravehearts" campaign with Keds kicks off and features particularly adorable shoes among her style picks.

FEBRUARY 2013

★ On February 10, Taylor celebrates the biggest night in music, picking up a Grammy for "Safe and Sound," opening the show with "Never Ever," and being the most enthusiastic audience member in the entire Staples Center by dancing and singing along to every artist's performance with pal Claire Kislinger.

★ On the Grammys red carpet in a J. Mendel gown, Taylor wore a diamond-and-amethyst bracelet by Jaimin, but what most style reporters didn't realize is that Jaimin is a pediatric cancer patient who had the chance to work with a famed jewelry designer to create a piece just for Taylor thanks to the Gabrielle's Angels Foundation. Beyoncé, Katy Perry, and Miley Cyrus also wore pieces from the philanthropic project. The young designer wanted the bracelet to sparkle because "Taylor sparkles."

★ At the BRIT Awards on the 20th, Taylor brings the house down with "I Knew You Were Trouble," but loses International Female Solo Artist to Lana Del Ray.

★ Taylor records a performance for British charity Comic Relief while in the U.K.

★ The Kids' Choice Awards show Taylor more love with three nominations: Favorite Female Singer, Favorite Song for "We Are Never Ever Getting Back Together," and Favorite Voice from an Animated Movie for *The Lorax*.

★ The ACM nominations have Taylor up for Entertainer of the Year, Album of the Year (as both artist and producer), Video of the Year ("We Are Never Ever Getting Back Together"), and Female Vocalist of the Year.

SEEING *RED*

Before *Red* had even been released, Swifties were eagerly anticipating Taylor's tour in support of the album. Never one to keep her fans waiting, Taylor made the announcement that she'd be hitting the road in her prime-time special *All Access Nashville with Katie Couric* just days after *Red*'s release. The Red Tour would kick off with a North American leg on March 13, 2013, an auspicious date for the "13" obsessed songstress. When tickets went on sale in November 2012, every seat in the house for the arena and stadium tour was snapped up in mere minutes — two shows in Los Angeles sold out in one minute alone! — and Taylor added additional shows to meet the huge demand.

Joining her on the road was "Everything Has Changed" co-writer Ed Sheeran, the British troubadour whose own star rose significantly in 2012, and Taylor also announced additional opening acts Austin Mahone, Joel Crouse, Brett Eldredge, Florida Georgia Line, and Casey James. Taylor's band, "The Agency," was of course back with her (including new drummer Matt Billingslea), as well as a troupe of over a dozen dancers, whom Taylor and Andrea Swift auditioned and chose from a group of over 400 hopefuls in early 2013. Also joining the Sparkly One onstage were her backup singers, whom fans first saw with Taylor in the MTV VMAs performance of "We Are Never Ever Getting Back Together."

Planning for the Red Tour started back in the summer of 2012, with Taylor putting in the same thoughtfulness and dedication that had made her previous headlining tours favorites. She didn't want this tour to be same-old, same-old for her true blue fans: she wanted to surprise. "I love for you to see a different thing for each song," said Taylor. "I love for there to be surprises — having the audience think they're going to see one thing and then it's a completely different thing than you thought. That's a really rewarding part of putting on a show."

While the Speak Now Tour was a huge success, Taylor worked hard to plan a tour for *Red* that suited the album. Choosing which songs from her four-album catalog made the set list had to wait until after *Red*'s release, because Taylor was keen to see which tracks were "the ones the fans are freaking out over the most, and those are the ones that are definitely in the set list." When it came to the visuals, Taylor wanted to switch it up: "I really wanted this tour to look completely different from the Speak Now Tour. I was so proud of the Speak Now Tour [but] I wanted this to have a different vibe." Discussing the differences between the two while prepping for the Red Tour, Taylor said, "The way that I look at the visuals for the Speak Now Tour is [that] it was very fantasy oriented, a very princessy vibe; it was much more straight-up theater. With this Red Tour . . . I think [it will be] more of a concert experience. There may be some elements of theater, but it's going to look more like this record looks. You'll have some costumes, but not all costumes. Like maybe a few less gowns. There won't be costume-costumes, but more like outfits. That's a girly thing to say though."

Taylor's focus was on the fans, as she told *Billboard*: "If we can make a show that dazzles people more than the last tour, then I'll have done my job in the right way. I just want to be able, in this economy, to make a show that for fans is definitely a guarantee that they will be entertained enough to warrant them leaving their house, spending their evening with me, parking their car, waiting in line, maybe buying a T-shirt. I want them to be so happy that they decided to spend their time with me . . . I really like to take people to a different world and change things up constantly, never showing them too much of the same thing too many times in a row."

For fans who wanted to see Taylor prepping for the big show, her new endorsement deal with Diet Coke – one of the tour's sponsors, along with Keds and American Greetings – provided a backstage pass with making-of videos released on the day of the tour's kickoff in Omaha, Nebraska. Taylor also made sure her loyal fans were taken care of, offering exclusive "best seat in the house" tickets for the pit directly in front of the Red Tour's red stage to members of Taylor Connect, Taylor's official fan community.

Taylor's new tour kept up old traditions: Momma and Papa Swift were seen walking through the crowd, handing out Red Tour guitar picks, lucky fans were invited to meet Taylor after the show at "Club Red" (the new name for the T Party room), attendees dressed up in video-inspired costumes (including the "Never Ever" furry animal suits), and there was a B stage at the other end of the arena. But the show had also matured along with Taylor, a fact she not-so-subtly winked at by playing "American Woman" before the show instead of the Speak Now Tour's "American Girl." In top vocal form, Taylor also joined Paul Sidoti for a guitar solo ("Red"), played the drums ("Holy Ground"), the piano ("All Too Well"), and even the 12-string guitar ("Sparks Fly"), the instrument she first learned to play on.

Taylor's refrain for the Red Tour was all about the fans and the unexpected – "whether it was taking a song that [fans] knew we'd play and kind of reformulating the song to sound different than they'd expected, or a different visual than they expected, or one minute you're seeing this outfit and a split second later it's this outfit" – and she was determined to deliver a night out to remember. "I really like to think that a good concert can be like a good book: it can take you away, it can take you to a different place and help you escape," said Taylor shortly before the tour began. "I think that's the main goal for me – helping the fans to escape, if only just for one night."

The superstar did have one other thing she wanted to do on each and every stop of the Red Tour, and that was to "walk out on stage every night and thank the fans for giving me the best year."

PHOTO NOTES & CREDITS

Front Cover At the iHeartRadio Music Festival on Sep. 22, 2012. (Scott Kirkland/PictureGroup)

p. ii Performing a sold-out show at Madison Square Garden on Aug. 27, 2009 (Theo Wargo/WireImage for *New York Post*/Getty Images)

p. 1 At the Candies Foundation Annual Event to Prevent benefit on May 7, 2008. (Eckstein/Retna Digital)

p. 2 Taylor photographed in 1994. (Andrew Orth/Retna)

p. 5 Taylor, age 11, with Berks Youth Theatre's Cody Derespina, Chris Brossman, and Jessica Flamholz in Mar. 2001. (Diane Staskowski, *The Reading Eagle*)

p. 6 Taylor's photo was in her local paper after she won a statewide poetry contest. (*The Reading Eagle*)

p. 8, 11 Taylor in 2004. Note the "I Heart ?" on her hand on p. 8. (Andrew Orth/Retna)

p. 13 In Nashville on Apr. 10, 2006. (John Shearer/WireImage/Getty Images)

p. 14 Leaving Wyomissing for Nashville. (*The Reading Eagle*)

p. 17 Photographed on May 2, 2000. (Reed Saxon/AP Photo)

p. 20 At the 52nd Annual Grammy Awards pre-telecast show. (Kevin Winter/Getty Images)

p. 23 Backstage at the 44th Annual ACMs on Apr. 5, 2009. (Frazer Harrison/ACM2009/Getty Images)

p. 25 In Nashville on Oct. 19, 2006. (Mark Humphrey/AP Photo)

p. 26 At the 44th Annual ACMs on Apr. 5, 2009. (Jae C. Hong/AP Photo)

p. 28 At a taping for Fox News on Oct. 25, 2006. (Michael Simon/startraksphoto.com)

p. 29 At *The Morning Show with Mike and Juliet* on Mar. 13, 2007. (Bill Davila/startraksphoto.com)

p. 31 In L.A. on Nov. 5, 2008. (Damian Dovarganes/AP Photo)

p. 33 At the 42nd Annual ACMs. (Mark J. Terrill/AP Photo)

p. 35 At the 41st ACMs on May 23, 2006. (Jacob Andrzejczak/Shooting Star)

p. 37 At the 41st CMA nominations on Aug. 30, 2007. (Barry McCloud/Shooting Star)

p. 41 Performing "Should've Said No" on May 18, 2008. (Mark J. Terrill/AP Photo)

p. 42 Arriving at the 40th Annual CMAs on Nov. 6, 2006. (Chitose Suzuki/AP Photo)

p. 45 Performing in Atlanta on Sep. 20, 2007. (Robb D. Cohen/Retna)

p. 46 Performing near her hometown. (Susan L. Angstadt, *The Reading Eagle*)

p. 47 At the 44th Annual ACMs on Apr. 5, 2009. (Dan Steinberg/AP Photo)

p. 48 Opening the 44th Annual ACMs. (Mark J. Terrill/AP Photo)

p. 50 Performing in Kansas City on May 11, 2007. (Jason Squires/WireImage/Getty Images)

p. 51 Arriving at the CMT Music Awards on Apr. 16, 2007. (Jason Moore/ZUMA Press/Keystone)

p. 52 Holding the Horizon Award at the 41st Annual CMAs on Nov. 7, 2007. (Peter Kramer/AP Photo)

p. 55 Performing at Stagecoach 2008 in Indio, CA, on May 3. (Jackie Butler/Retna)

p. 56 Performing on *Today* on May 29, 2009. (PseudoImage/Shooting Star)

p. 57 At her hometown Walmart in Hendersonville on Nov. 11, 2008. (Aaron Crisler/Retna)

p. 59 Performing during Country Thunder in Twin Lakes, WI, on Jul. 16, 2009. (Rob Grabowski/Retna)

p. 61 After Taylor and Miley's performance of "Fifteen." (John Shearer/WireImage/Getty Images)

p. 63 Performing at the 42nd Annual CMAs on Nov. 12, 2008. (Mark Humphrey/AP Photo)

p. 64 At a pre-Grammy party on Feb. 8, 2008. (Tony DiMaio/Shooting Star)

p. 69 At the Beverly Wilshire Hotel. (Sara De Boer/Retna)

p. 71 Joe Jonas and Taylor sing "Should've Said No" on Jul. 14, 2008, in Anaheim, CA. (Shelby Casanova)

p. 74 At the Sprint Sound & Speed event on Jan. 9, 2010. (Randi Radcliff/AdMedia/Keystone Press)

p. 75 Performing at Madison Square Garden on Aug. 27, 2009. (Stephen Chernin/AP Photo)

p. 77, 78 (top row), **79** (bottom right) The Fearless Tour in Lafayette, LA, on Sep. 11, 2009. (Mallory Bartow)

p. 78 (bottom three), **79** (all but bottom right), **80** The Fearless Tour in Indianapolis, IN, on Oct. 8, 2009. (Adam W. Lewis)

p. 83 At the CMA Awards on Nov. 11, 2009. (Sanford

Myers/*The Tennessean*/ZUMApress.com/Keystone Press)

p. 87 The Fearless Tour in Orlando, FL, on Mar. 5, 2010. (MavrixPhoto.com/Keystone Press)

p. 89 Arriving at the CMT Music Awards on Jun. 16, 2009. (Bill Davila/startraksphoto.com)

p. 91 Posing with her awards backstage at the 44th Annual ACMs on Apr. 5, 2009. (Jae C. Hong/AP Photo)

p. 92 Posing with her Grammys on Jan. 31, 2010. (Vince Bucci/PictureGroup/AP Images)

p. 94 Performing with Caitlin in Atlanta, GA, on Sep. 3, 2009. (James Palmer/Retna)

p. 95 Arriving at the 44th Annual CMA Awards on Nov. 10, 2010. (Bob Charlotte/PR Photos)

p. 96 In London, England, on Aug. 24, 2009. (wenn.com/Keystone Press)

p. 97 Outside the *Late Show with David Letterman* on Oct. 26, 2010. (Paul Froggatt/PR Photos)

p. 99 At *Time*'s 100 Most Influential People in the World gala on May 4, 2010. (Fernando Leon/Elevation/PictureGroup)

p. 101 Performing in Central Park, NYC, on Oct. 25, 2010. (Ken Katz/startraksphoto.com)

p. 102 Performing a surprise show at Hollywood and Highland in L.A. on Oct. 29, 2010. (Norman Scott/star traksphoto.com)

p. 104 Arriving at the Teen Choice Awards on Aug. 7, 2011. (Andrew Evans/PR Photos)

p. 107 Arriving at the American Music Awards on Nov. 20, 2011. (Al Ortega)

p. 109 Performing on the *Today Show* on Oct. 26, 2010. (Janet Mayer/PR Photos)

p. 110 Leaving the *Late Show with David Letterman* on Oct. 26, 2010. (Paul Froggatt/PR Photos)

p. 111 Arriving at the Billboard Music Awards on May 22, 2011. (Andrew Evans/PR Photos)

p. 113 The Speak Now Tour in Birmingham, U.K., on Mar. 22, 2011. (Solarpix/PR Photos)

p. 115 Arriving at the American Music Awards on Nov. 21, 2010. (David Gabber/PR Photos)

p. 116 In Nashville, TN, on Sep. 19, 2011. (Andrew Evans/PR Photos)

p. 117 Arriving at the American Music Awards on Nov. 18, 2012. (David Gabber/PR Photos)

p. 119 At the Christmas lights ceremony at Westfield Shopping Centre in London, U.K., on Nov. 6, 2012. (Landmark/PR Photos)

p. 121 Performing in Times Square, NYC, on Dec. 31,

2012. (Janet Mayer/PR Photos)

p. 122 At KIIS FM's 2012 Jingle Ball on Dec. 1, 2012. (David Gabber/PR Photos)

p. 127 Performing on *Good Morning America* on Oct. 23, 2012. (Janet Mayer/PR Photos)

p. 128 Ed Sheeran at *New.Music.Live* in Toronto, ON, on Sep. 17, 2012. (Robin Wong/PR Photos)

p. 129 Ethel Shakel Kennedy and Taylor at the premiere of *Ethel* at the 2012 Sundance Film Festival on Jan. 19, 2012. (Gary Neal/startraksphoto.com)

p. 131 Arriving at the MTV VMAs on Sep. 7, 2008. (Sthanlee B. Mirador/Shooting Star)

p. 133 In the pressroom at the 2007 CMT Music Awards. (Tammie Arroyo/AP Photo)

p. 134 Backstage on Apr. 14, 2008. (Rick Diamond/WireImage/Getty Images)

p. 136 Performing on Nov. 12, 2008. (ZUMAPRESS.com/Keystone Press)

p. 138 Lucas Till in Apr. 2009. (Albert Michael/startrak sphoto.com)

p. 139 Taylor and Andrea Swift arriving at the 42nd Annual ACMs on May 15, 2007. (Charles Santiago/Shooting Star)

p. 140 Arriving at the MTV VMAs on Sep. 6, 2012. (David Gabber/PR Photos)

p. 143 Performing "Mean" at the Grammys on Feb. 12, 2012. (Frank Micelotta/PictureGroup)

p. 144 Arriving at the People's Choice Awards on Jan. 9, 2013. (Andrew Evans/PR Photos)

p. 147 Backstage after performing at the MTV VMAs on Sep. 6, 2012. (Frank Micelotta/PictureGroup)

p. 149 At the *Hannah Montana: The Movie* premiere on Apr. 2, 2009. (Sthanlee B. Mirador/Shooting Star)

p. 150 Nick, Taylor Swift, Joe, and Kevin Jonas in *Jonas Brothers: The 3D Concert Experience*. (Frank Masi, Disney Enterprises, Inc./Fotos International/Keystone Press)

p. 151 With Demi Lovato at the *Hannah Montana: The Movie* premiere. (Matt Sayles/AP Photo)

p. 153 Filming in West L.A. on Jul. 30, 2009. (Fame Pictures, Inc./Keystone Press)

p. 154 Waiting to answer phones during the Hope for Haiti Now telethon in L.A. (MTV/Retna)

p. 155 Carrie Underwood, Kelly Pickler, and Taylor at a Nashville Predators game on Dec. 27, 2007. (Mike Strasinger/AdMedia/Keystone Press)

p. 156 At the premiere of *The Lorax* in Universal City, CA, on Feb. 19, 2012. (David Gabber/PR Photos)

© ECW Press, 2010, 2013

Published by ECW Press
2120 Queen Street East, Suite 200,
Toronto, Ontario, Canada M4E 1E2
416-694-3348 / info@ecwpress.com

LIBRARY AND ARCHIVES CANADA CATALOGUING IN PUBLICATION

Spencer, Liv
Taylor Swift / Liv Spencer. — Platinum ed.

ISBN 978-1-77041-151-7
ALSO ISSUED AS: 978-1-77090-405-7 (PDF); 978-1-77090-406-4 (EPUB)

Previously published under title: Taylor Swift : every day is a fairytale.

1. Swift, Taylor, 1989– —Juvenile literature. 2. Country musicians—
United States—Biography—Juvenile literature. I. Title.

ML3930.S977S74 2012   j782.42164092   C2012-907523-X

Text and photo editor: Crissy Boylan
Cover and interior design: Carolyn McNeillie
Production: Troy Cunningham

Thank you to the T-Swift fans who helped with photos of the Fearless Tour.
Special thank you to Jennifer Knoch and Crissy Calhoun: I had the time of
my life slaying dragons with you. — Liv

This book was printed in March 2013 at Courier, Kendallville, IN, USA.

The publication of *Taylor Swift: The Platinum Edition* has been
generously supported by the Government of Canada through
the Canada Book Fund.

Canadä